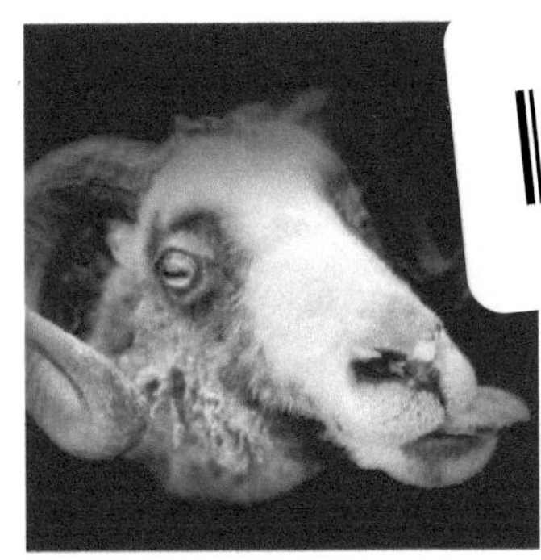

The Sheep of Celtic Herd-

Ewe Are Funny!

Roxanne Marie Dean

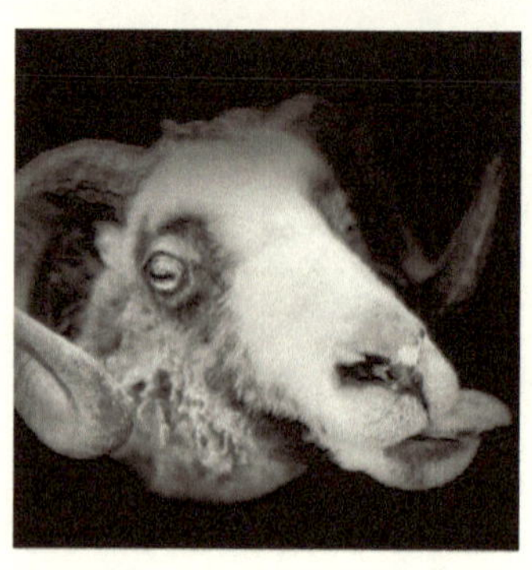

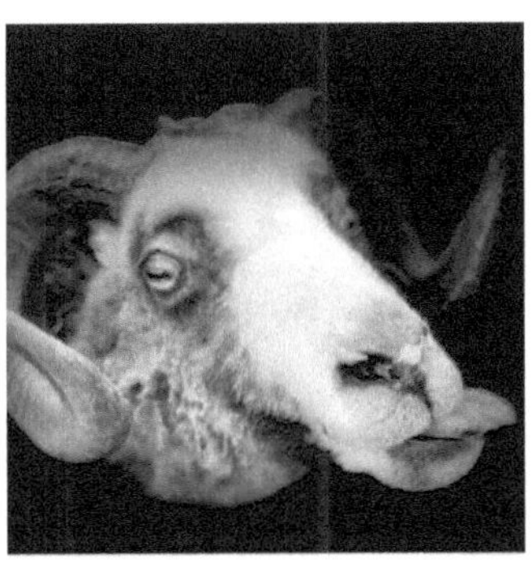

DEDICATION

This book is dedicated to a friend and sheep mentor that passed away way too soon! Her knowledge and friendship will always be appreciated and treasured.
Kathleen Byrne Davidson with Harley-The Australian Shepherd who has his own series of books!

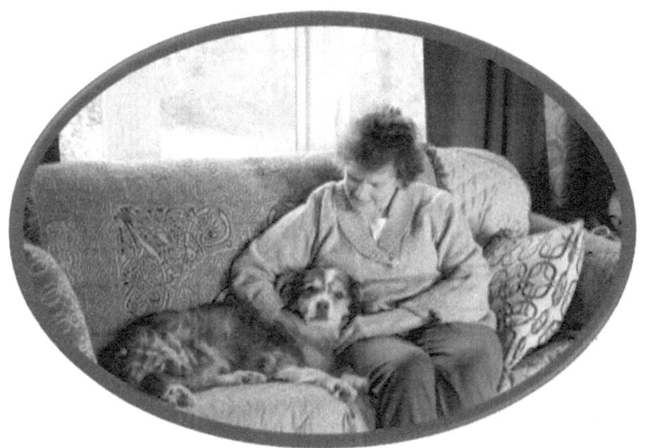

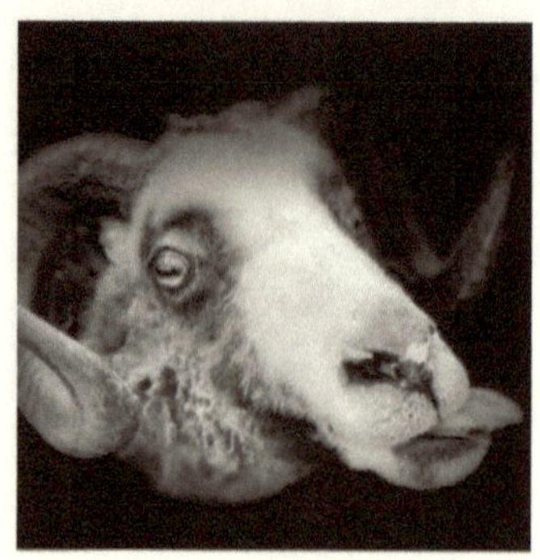

CONTENTS

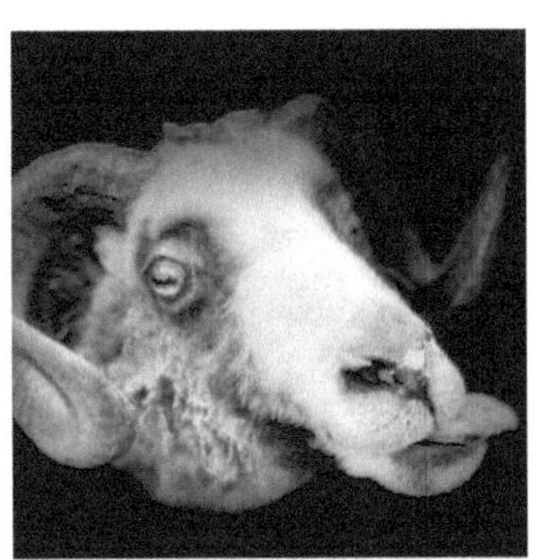

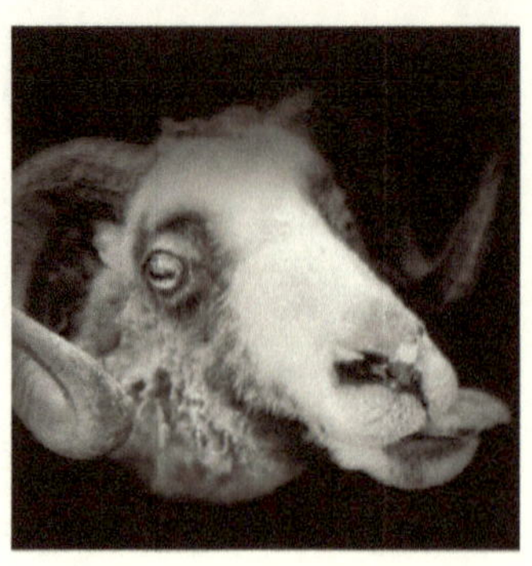

ACKNOWLEDGMENTS

This is the third book about Celtic Herd Sheep based on Scottish Sheep starting with "Sheila The Sheep," who was the alpha ewe of this bunch and the smartest sheep I have ever owned!

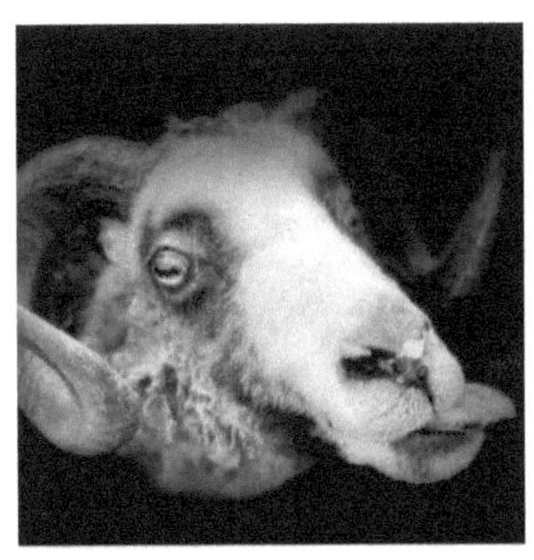

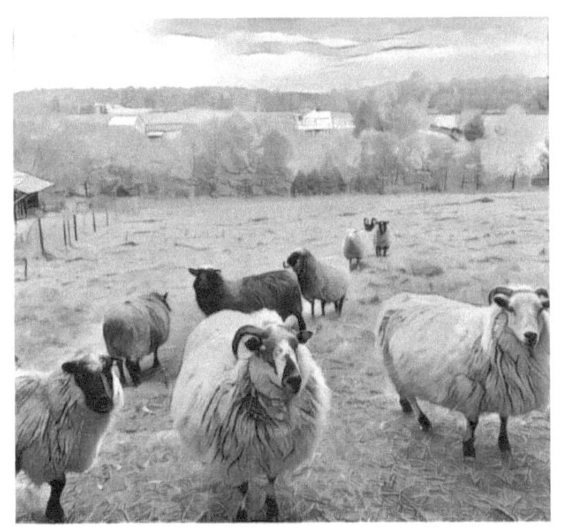

Scottish Sheep

1

There are several varieties of Scottish Blackface
found in the United Kingdom,
Scotland, Devon, Cornwall, and Northern Ireland.
Blackfaces are horned with a black face but can
have white markings on the face also. They can
also have black legs. The breed is mostly raised
for meat since their wool can be very coarse

although it is used in Harris Tweed.
You need hundreds of pounds of the wool in order to make a Harris Tweed Jacket.
The breed is primarily a British breed of sheep. It is the most common sheep breed of the United Kingdom. However, it did not originate in Scotland but south of the border!

Blackface ewes are excellent mothers and great protectors of their offspring. They are great producers of milk, even when on marginal pastures and are able to produce lambs on hillsides.

During the 1900's, the breed spread rapidly to the highlands and the islands and also to Northern Ireland and the US. In the USA it is only considered a minor breed. The Scottish Blackface sheep can survive on brushy hillsides and are instrumental for improving pastures.

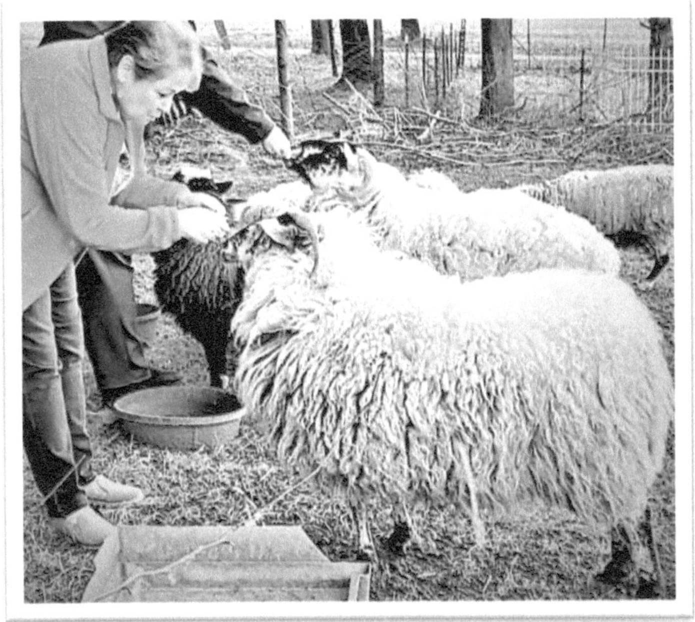

Scottish Blackface Sheep at "Celtic Herd" enjoy cookies from visitors

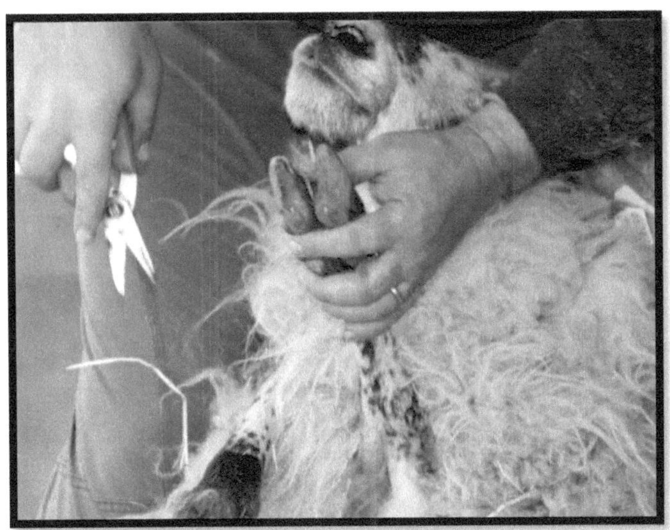

Hooves Clipped

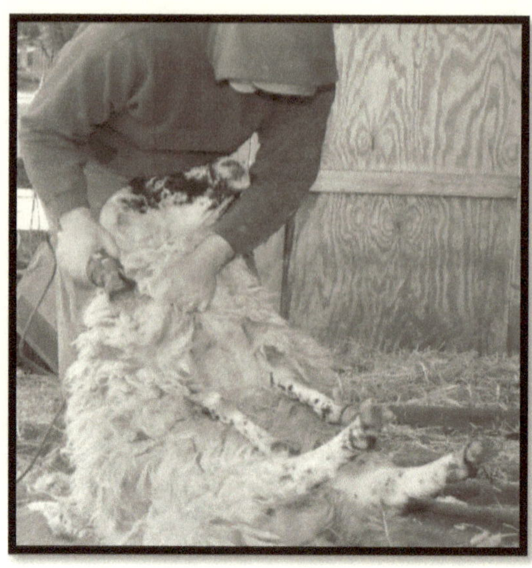

Shearing Time
Scottish blackface Ewe

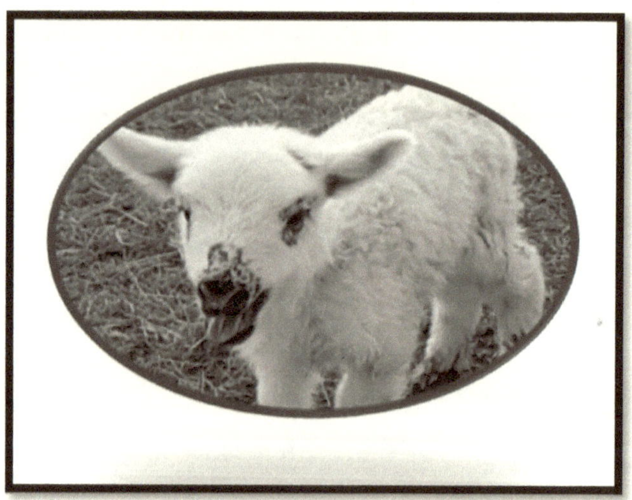

Lambs Start Out With Minimal Markings

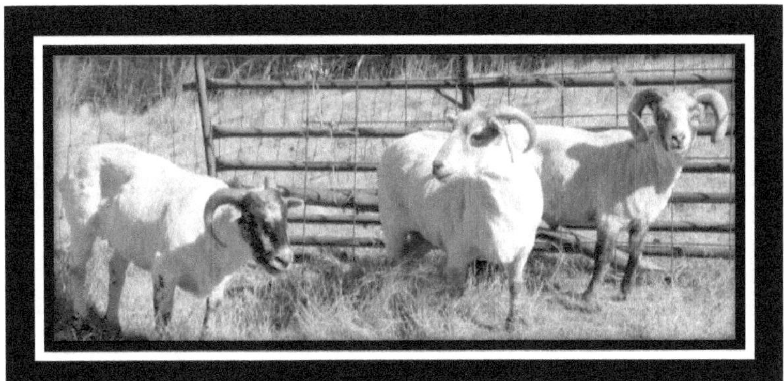

Sheared Sheep

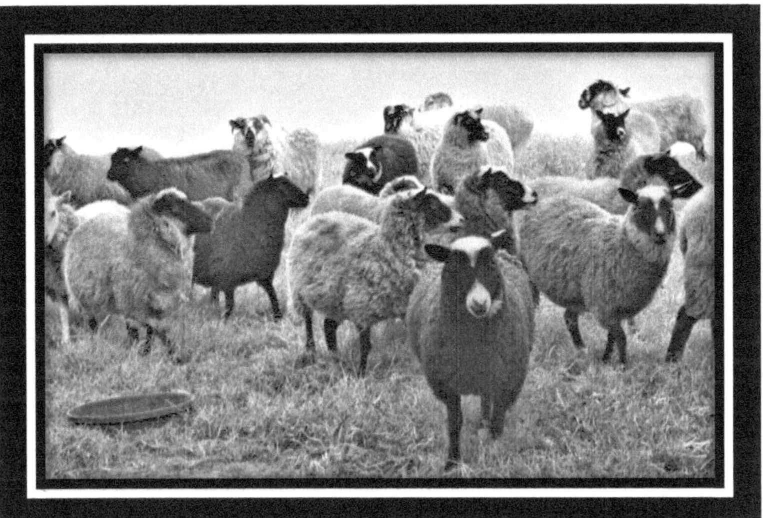

Celtic Herd Farm by R.Dean

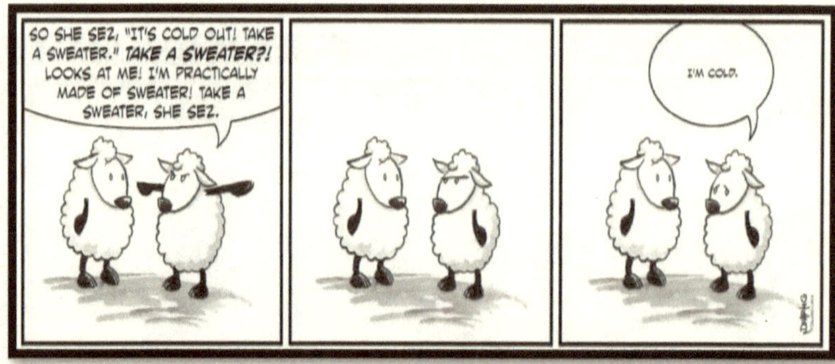

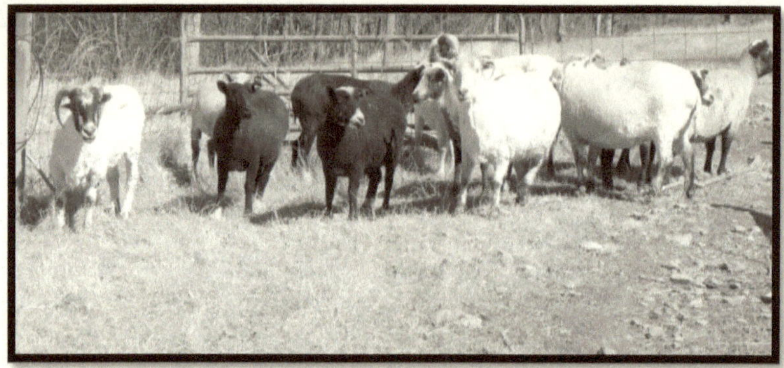

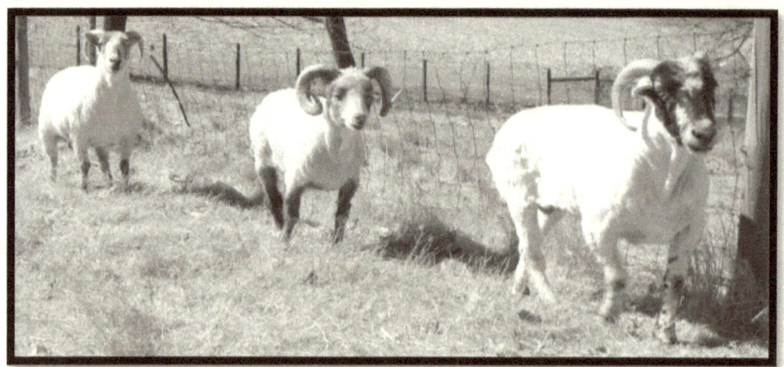

Lisa Scottish Blackface Ewe in Front

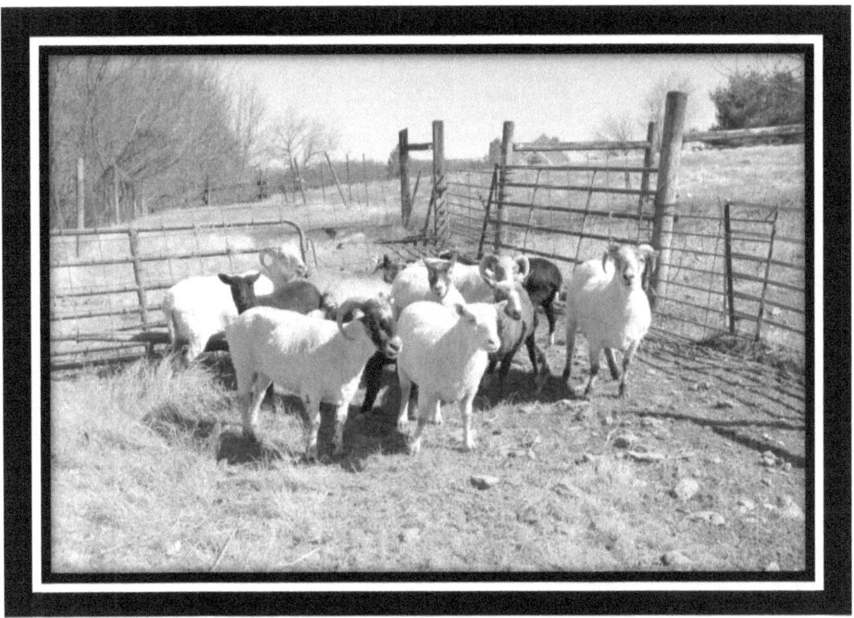

Herding Together After Being Sheared

Ewe look a lot thinner, your muscles are firm,
Ewe seem to be care-free and done with your
Squirms.
The wool got to be heavy at least 5-6 pounds
Ewe don't look so hefty, not nearly so round.
Ewe run a lot faster, so happy and free
It's different this feeling -your thinking, it's me?
Yes you lost lots of weight, but thank ewe so much!
That stuff ewe just shredded will spin into a bunch!
The yarn will be lovely, and what can it make?
Sweaters, scarves and stockings – Wow that's great!

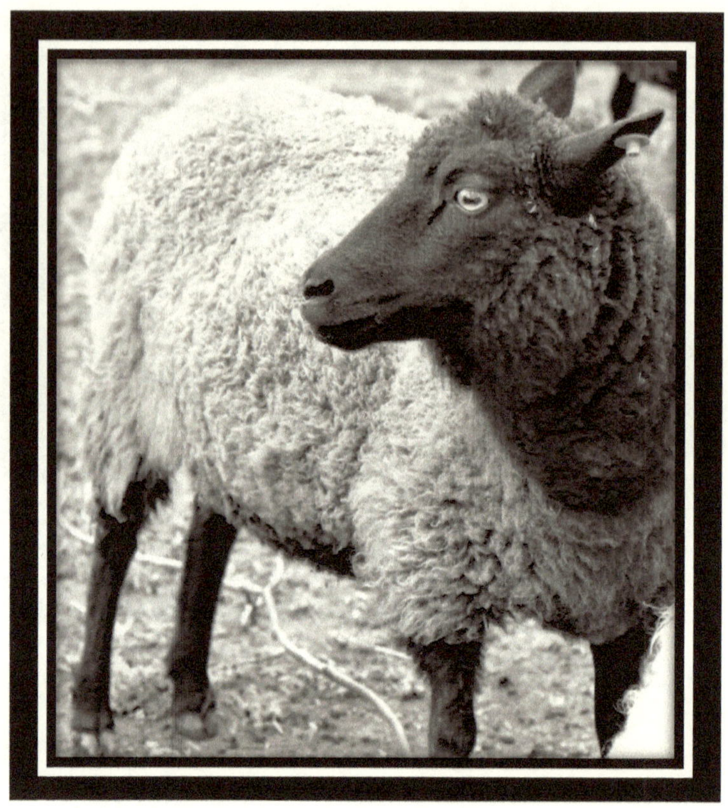

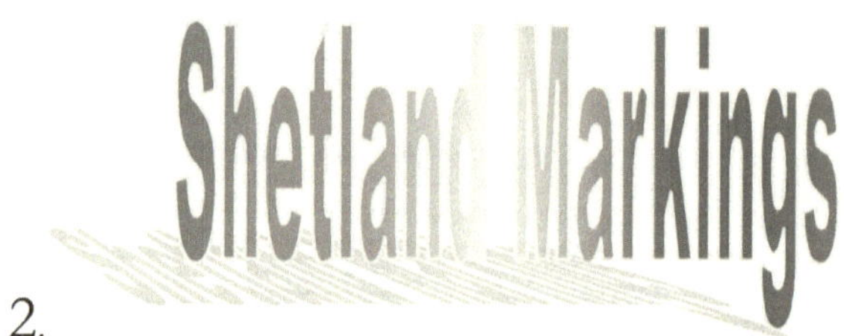

2.

Shetland Ewe

Ewe seem to be two colors, ewe aren't like all the rest. Your head and neck are darker then the back of you -what the heck?

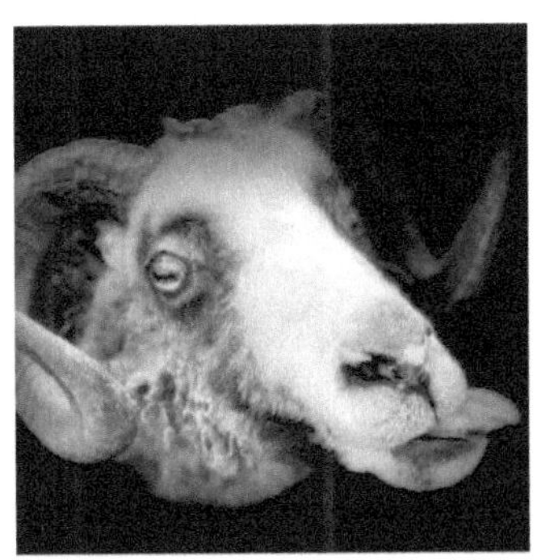

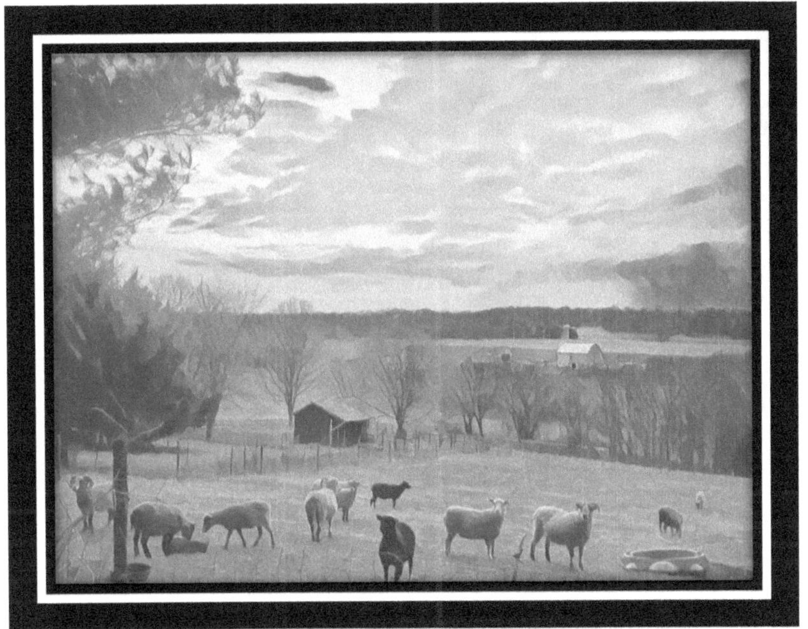

Shetland Tails

The tail is a good indicator of whether or not a particular sheep is a purebred Shetland. The Shetland is a member of the European short-

tailed breed with a wool covered, fluke-
shaped tail that is normally 4 to 5 inches long .

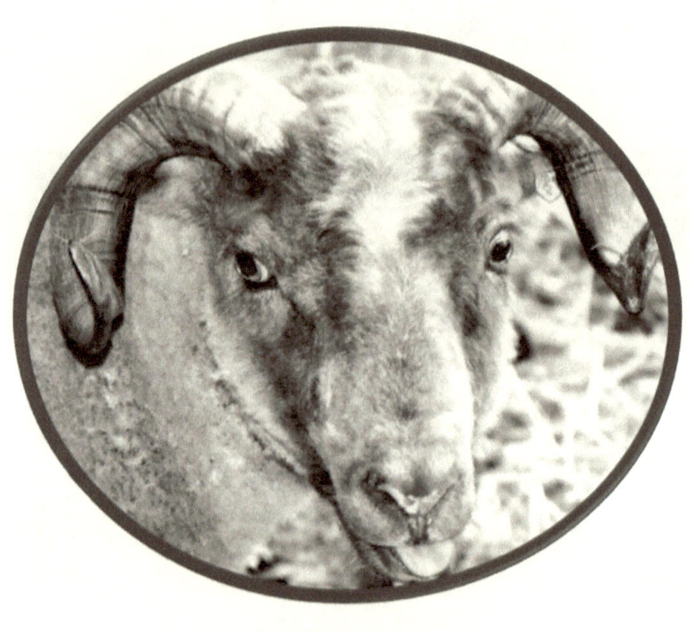

Moorit Shetland Ram

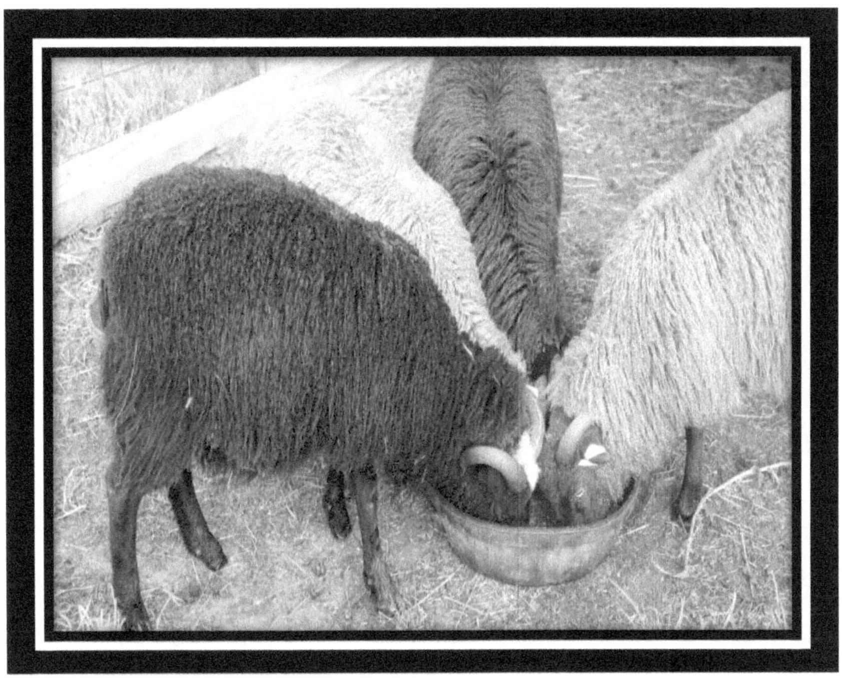

Shetlands have a natural colored fleece. The black one in the front has white on the top of his head.

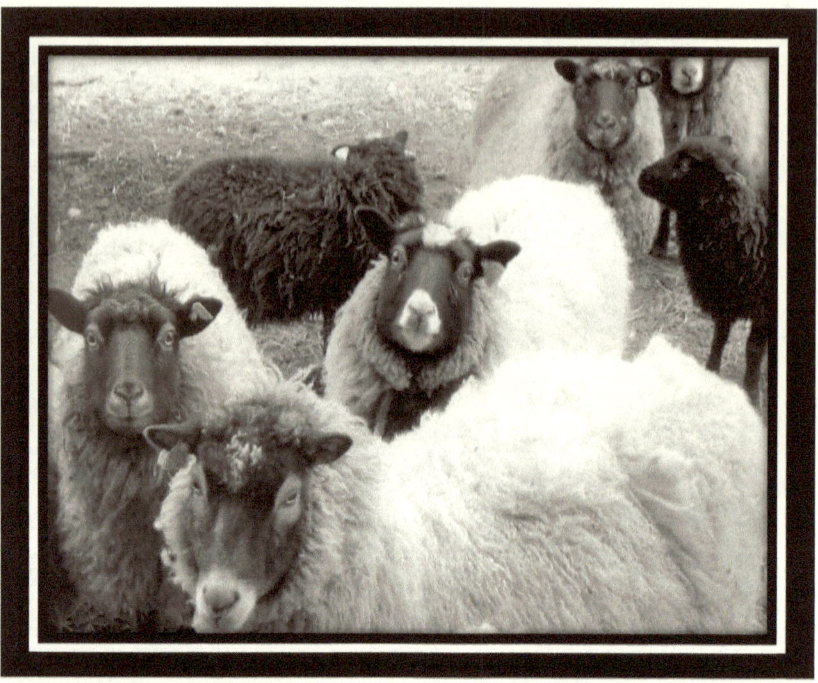

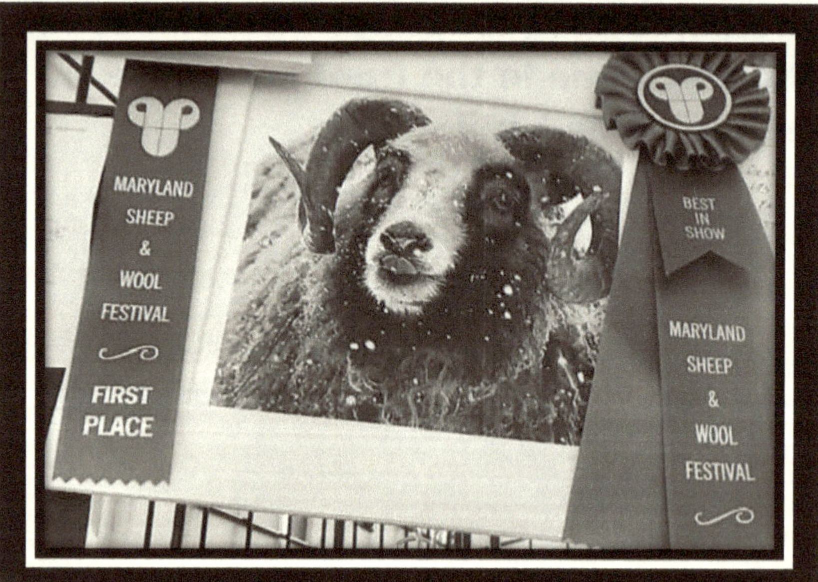

Celtic Herd Shetlands

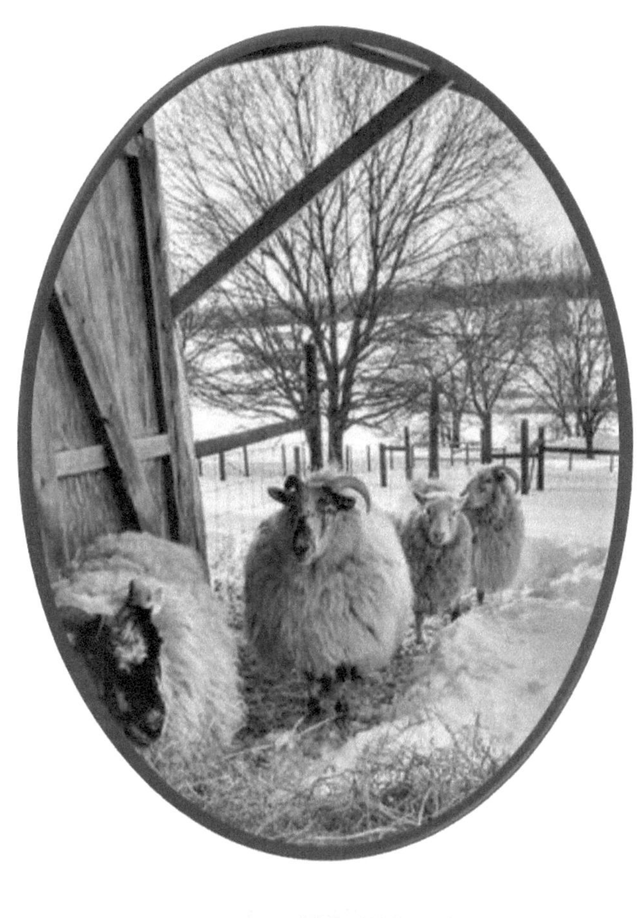

Scottish Blackface Ewes have horns but Shetland EWES Don't!

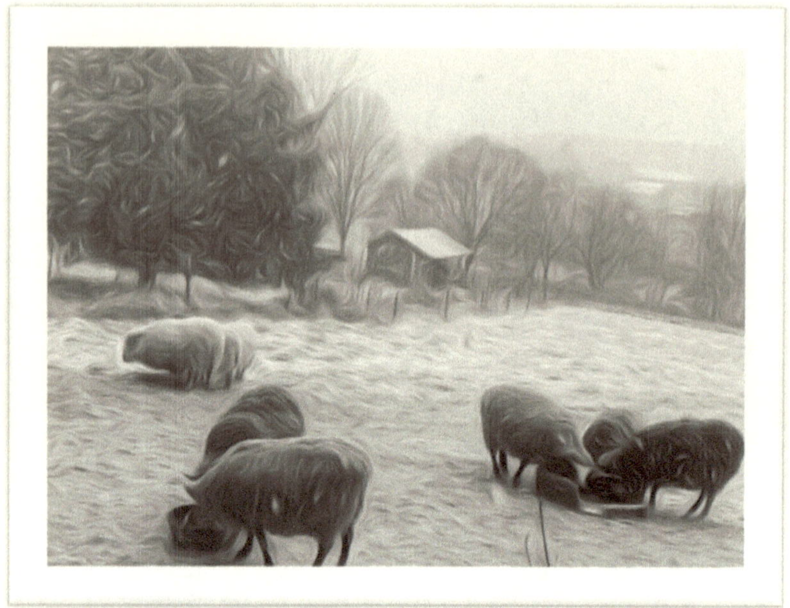

Abstract Photo Celtic Herd Farm

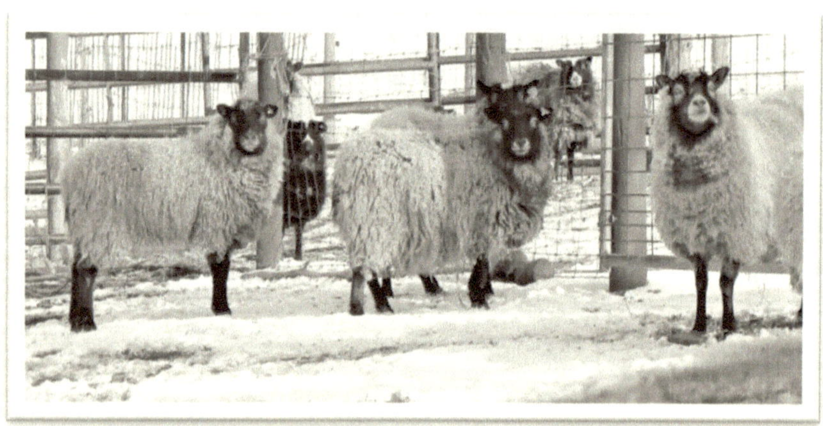

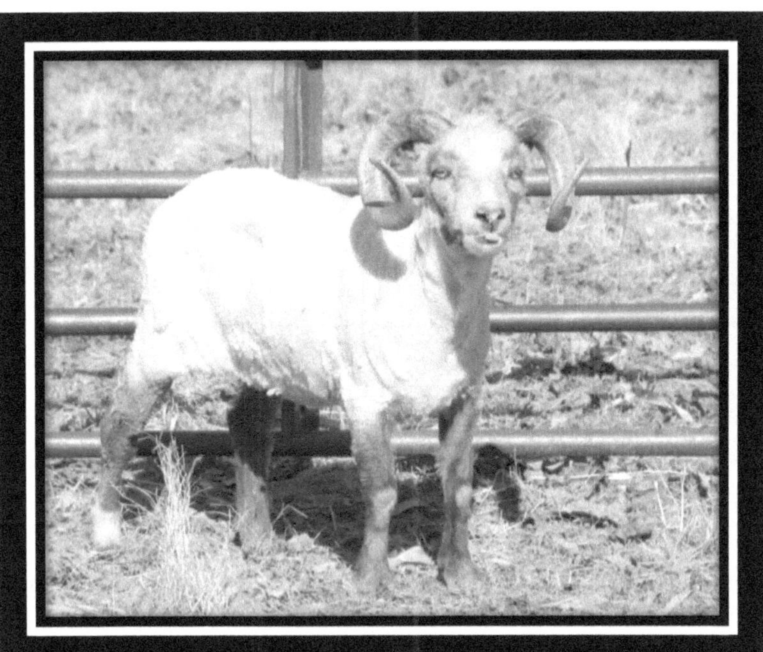

Shetland Ram Sheared- by R.Dean

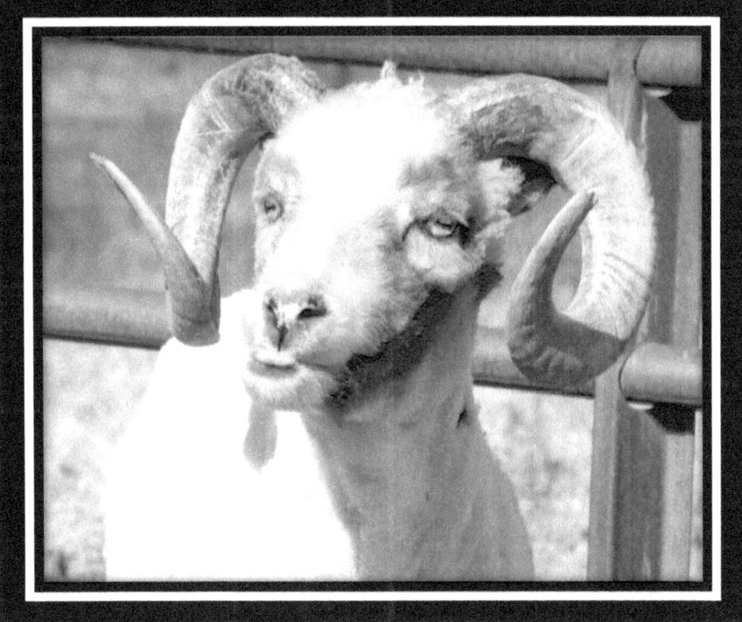

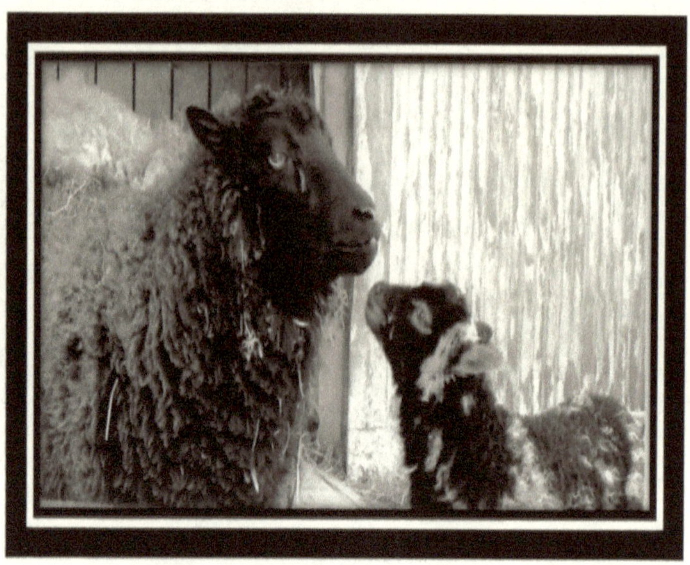

Lambs are born with spots that merge into a solid color after about six months. This Ram Lamb became all black except for around the eyes!

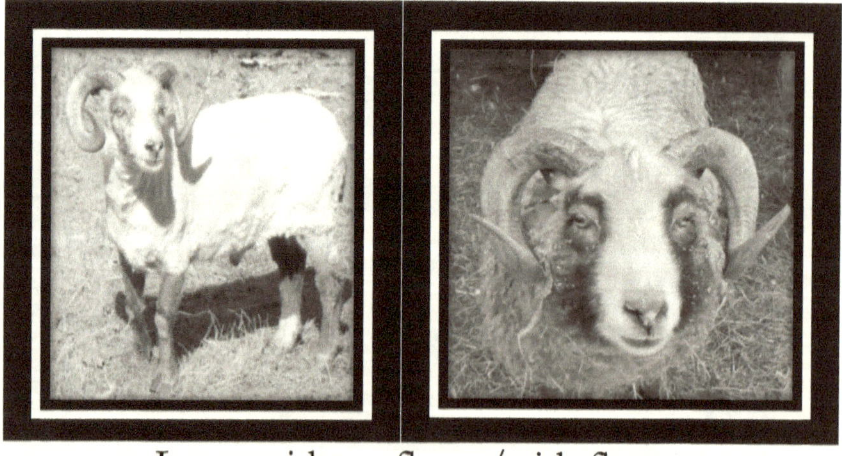

Laggy without fleece/with fleece

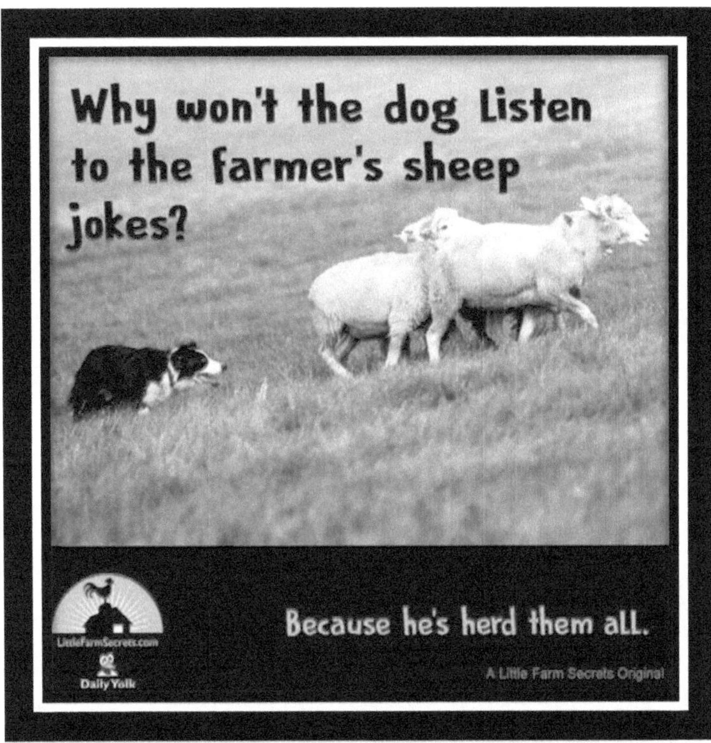
Why won't the dog listen
to the farmer's sheep
jokes?
Because he's herd them all.
LittleFarmSecrets.com
Daily Yolk
A Little Farm Secrets Original

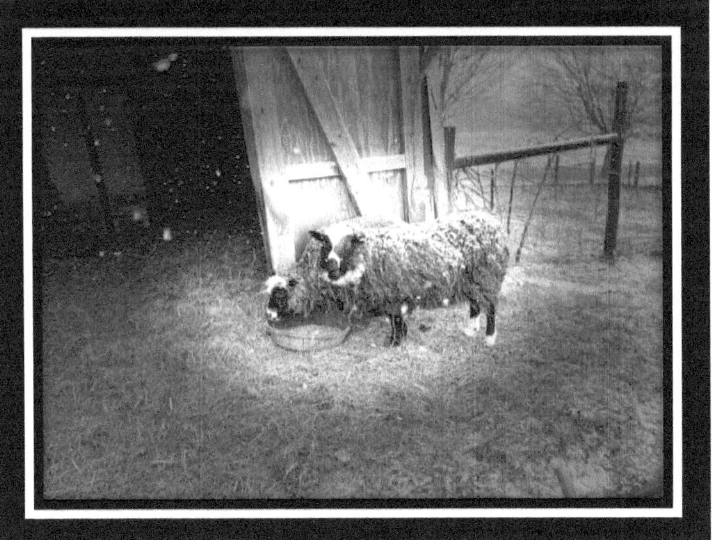

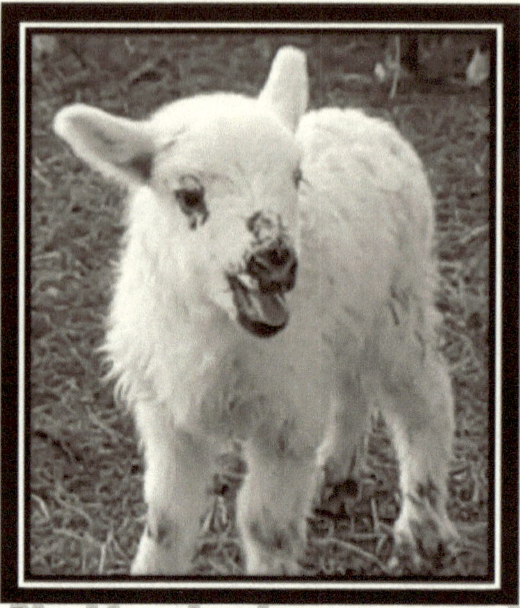

Scottish Blackface Lambs are very verbal!

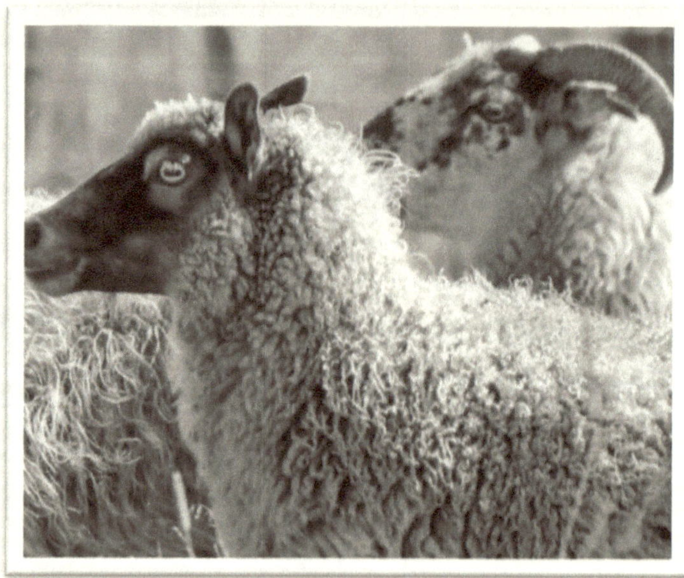

Shetland and Scottish Blackface Ewes

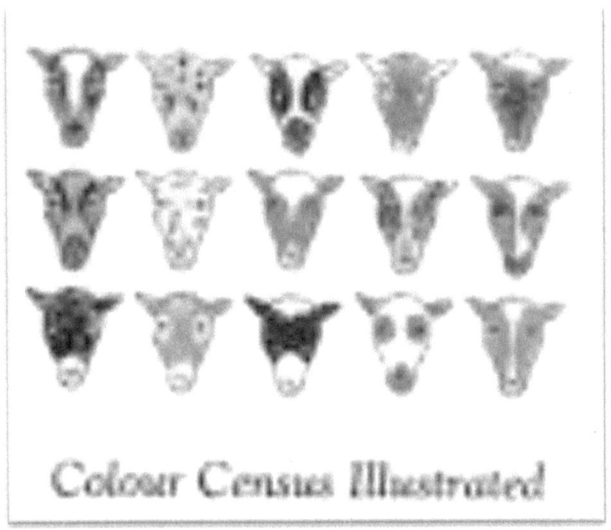

Shetland Markings

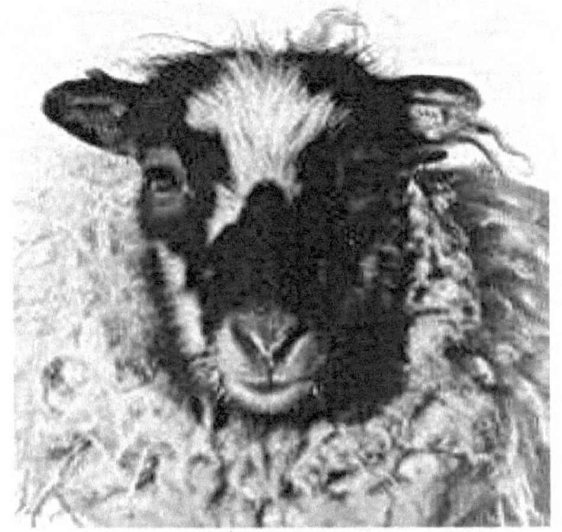

grey smirslet

Shetlands have a broad variety of colors and markings. The names used to describe markings are the original ones used by the Shetland Islanders. They include the following list:

- **Bersugget** – irregular patches of different colors; variegated markings

- <u>Bielset</u> – having a complete circular band of different color around neck.
- **Bioget** – with white back and darker sides and belly, or conversely,
- **Blaeget** – having a lighter shade on the outer part of the wool fiber, especially in moorit and dark brown sheep.
- <u>Blaget</u> – white with irregular dark patches resembling ground partly snow covered.
- **Blettet** – with white spots on nose and top of head.
- <u>Bleset</u> – dark colored with white stripe down the forehead,
- **Brandet** – having stripes of another color across body.

- **Bronget – dark colored with light-colored breast, or conversely,**
- **<u>Flecket</u> – white with large black or brown patches (not as well defined as in Jacob sheep).**
- **<u>Fronet</u> – black-spotted with white head and black spots around eyes.**
- **<u>Gulmoget</u> – having light under parts with dark-colored body; opposite of katmoget.**
- **<u>Ilget</u> – white with spots of a different color (usually grey or black).**
- **<u>Iset</u> – dark colored with many white fibres giving bluish hue from a distance.**
- **<u>Katmoget</u> – having a light colored body with dark belly and legs, and moget facial markings.**
- **Katmollet – having light-colored nose and jaws.**
- **Kraiget – having neck of different color from rest of body.**
- **Kranset – dark colored with white around eyes and neck.**
- **Krunet – dark colored with white patch on top of head.**
- **Marlit – various shades of different colors, mottled.**

- **Moget** – characteristic dark and light patches around mouth, eyes, and ears.
- **<u>Mirkface</u>** – white with dark patches on face.
- **Mullit** – white with dark nose and jaws, or conversely,
- **Sholmet** – of any color, other than white, with a white face.
- **Skeget** – stripes of different colors on sides.
- **<u>Smirslet</u>** – dark colored with white around the mouth, head or neck
- **<u>Sokket</u>** – with legs of a different color from that of the body.
- **<u>Sponget</u>** – dark colored with small white spots, or conversely,
- **Snaelit** – light-colored with snow-white face.
- **<u>Yuglet</u>** – having color around eyes different from remainder of body.

Found in : <u>Shetland Markings - NASSA</u>

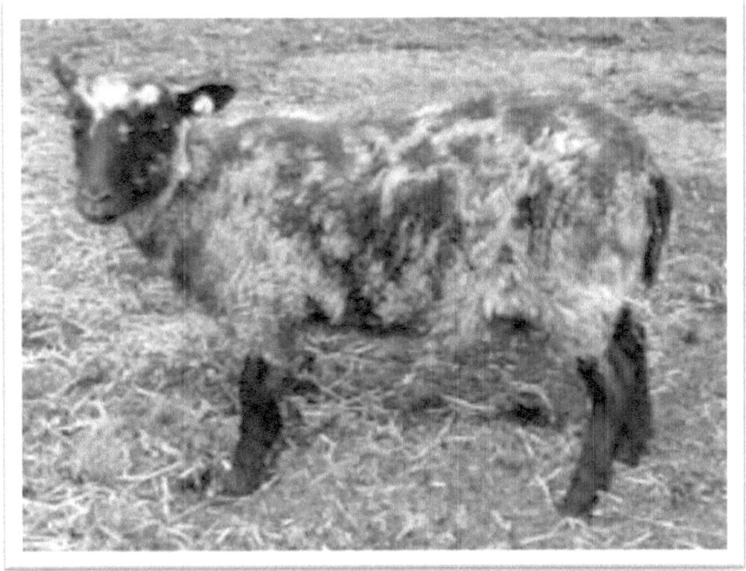

Blaget

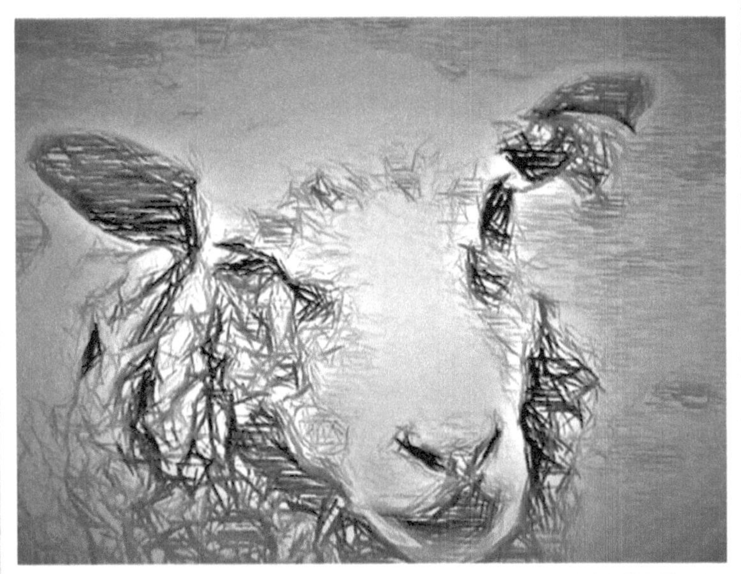

Abstract Ewe by R.Dean

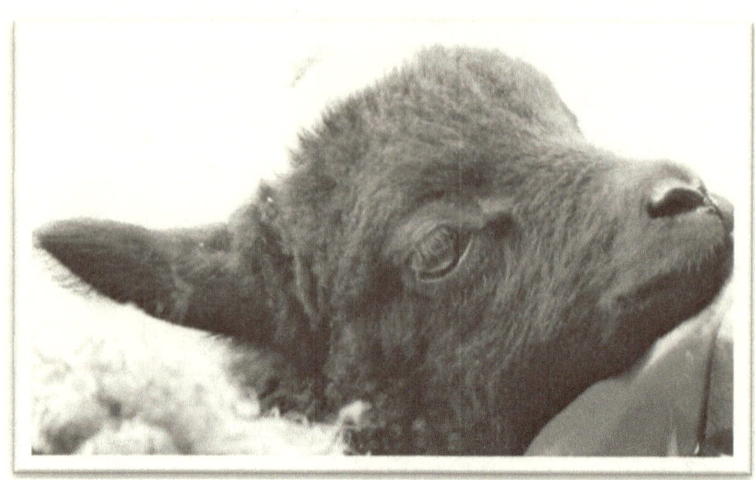

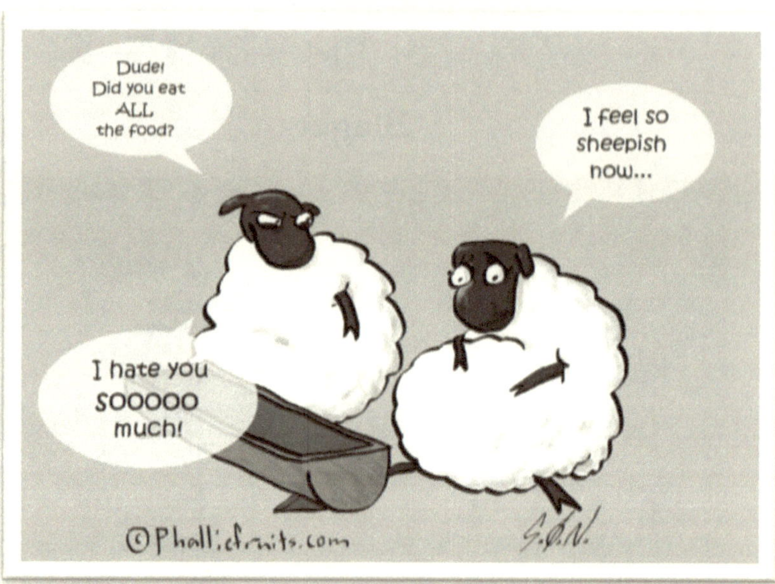

Dude!
Did you eat
ALL
the food?
I feel so
sheepish
now...
I hate you
SOOOOO
much!
©Phallicfruits.com

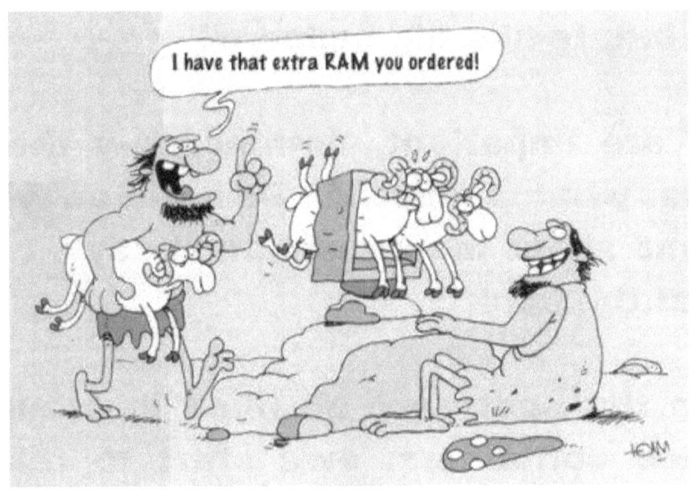

Ewe like it when I come down the hill with a bucket of sheep feed.

I notice that you're smiling and can't wait to take care of your needs!

Your faces start to light up in anticipation, and your pace -wow- it begins to quicken! You start planning how your mouth will start to thicken!

Your expressions do amuse me -you are chomping at the bit. You squirm around and try to find that spot that you can fit!

The bigger you are you can take up more room.

While the rest of ewe have to squeeze

in and inflate like big balloons!

Ewe are impatient, nothing new there
That is what I expect. Sometimes you
push and shove me around and I say
"What the heck"!

Once the spots are all filled in around
the feed containers, ewe start to relax
and enjoy the meal without listening to
the ewes-usual complainers!

Finally it's all gone and the feed has
been dispursed.
Some of you piggies start to choke and
ewe are not the worse!
Then it's time to rest a bit and find a
spot to drop. Spreading out around the hill
until you finally stop!

Do ewe start planning for when the next
time comes around?
Or are you so full for now that ewe
simply hit the ground?

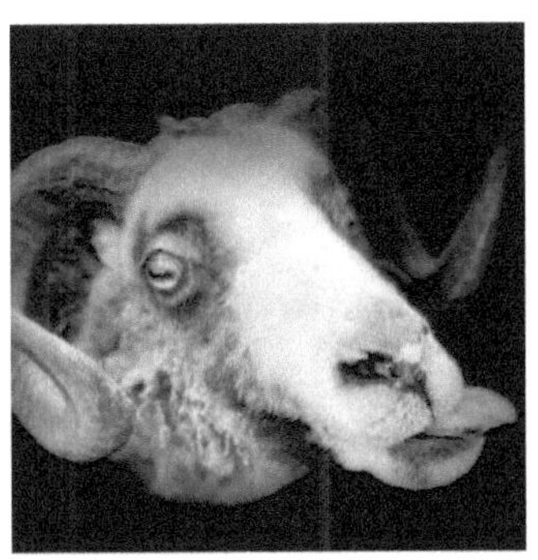

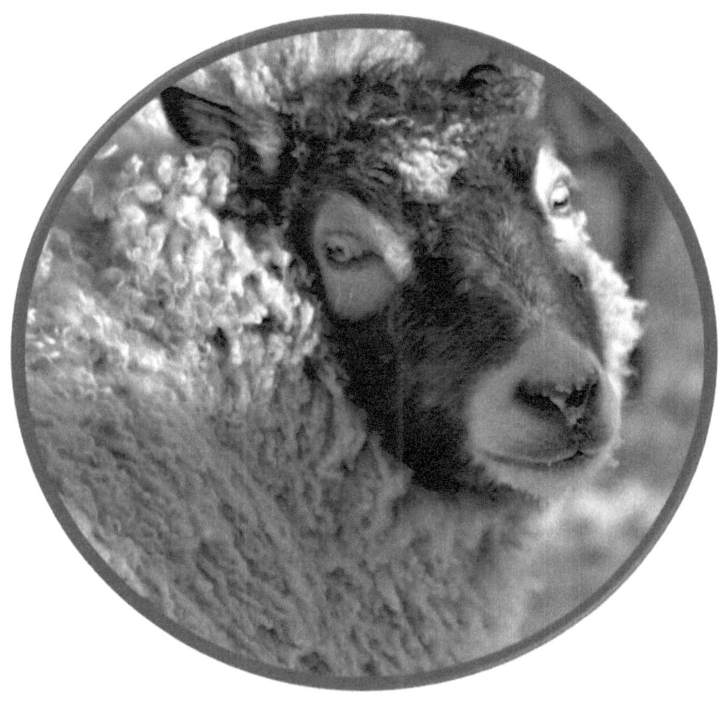

Celtic Herd Shetland Ewe

Shetland Colors

Shetlands have more color combinations than any other bred of sheep.

<u>White</u>
<u>Greys to Black</u> (listed from light to dark)
- **Light Grey**
- **Grey**
- **Emsket – dusky bluish-grey**
- **Shaela – dark steely-grey, like black frost**
- **Black**

<u>Browns</u> (listed from light to dark)
- **Musket – light greyish-brown**
- **Fawn**
- **Mioget – light moorit (yellowish-brown)**
- **Moorit – shades between fawn and dark reddish brown**
- **Dark Brown**

Source: North American Shetland Sheep Association

SHEILA THE SHEEP

3

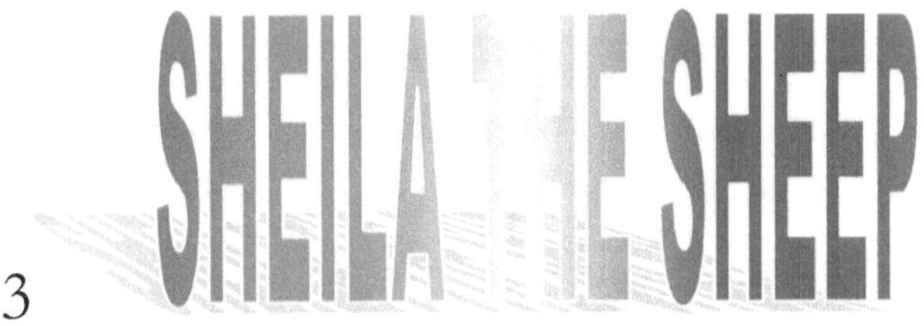

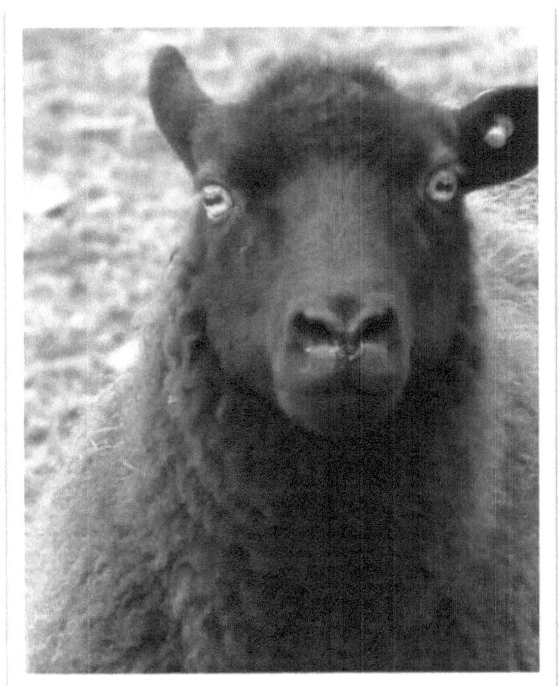

Sheila The Shetland Ewe

Sheila was the Shetland Ewe who was a smart one and this is True!

She kept the moms and lambs quite safe. She whistled to them when they

needed to change their pace.

She was quick to manage the situations at hand. It didn't matter if it was a mom or a lamb.

She was friendly to people right from the start. You couldn't help love her with all of your heart!

The stories about her came with lots of information. You can certainly say she was my inspiration!

Sheila was a Shetland Ewe, a Scottish creature who didn't Moo!

Her baaa could be heard all over the farm, she followed you around like she was part of your arm.

Her line of sheep were special too, Some are still here and continue to roo!

What joy they bring in all four seasons, I write about them for many reasons!

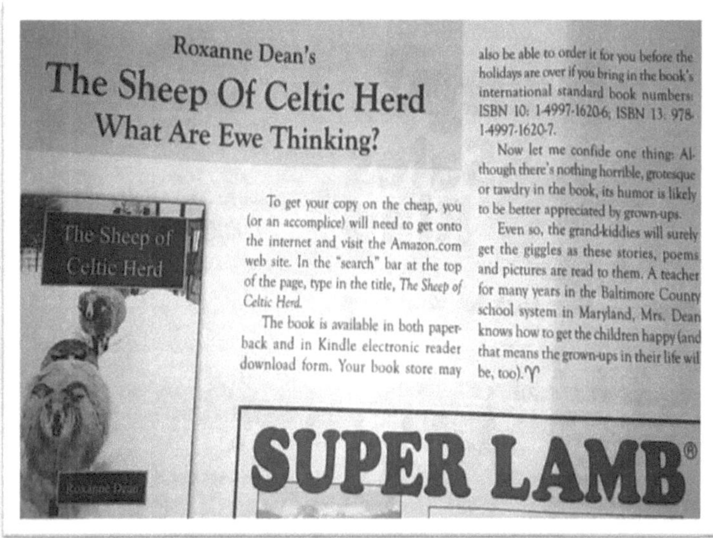

Roxanne Dean's

The Sheep Of Celtic Herd
What Are Ewe Thinking?

To get your copy on the cheap, you (or an accomplice) will need to get onto the internet and visit the Amazon.com web site. In the "search" bar at the top of the page, type in the title, *The Sheep of Celtic Herd.*

The book is available in both paperback and in Kindle electronic reader download form. Your book store may also be able to order it for you before the holidays are over if you bring in the book's international standard book numbers: ISBN 10: 1-4997-1620-6; ISBN 13: 978-1-4997-1620-7.

Now let me confide one thing: Although there's nothing horrible, grotesque or tawdry in the book, its humor is likely to be better appreciated by grown-ups.

Even so, the grand-kiddies will surely get the giggles as these stories, poems and pictures are read to them. A teacher for many years in the Baltimore County school system in Maryland, Mrs. Dean knows how to get the children happy (and that means the grown-ups in their life will be, too).

Article from Sheep Magazine

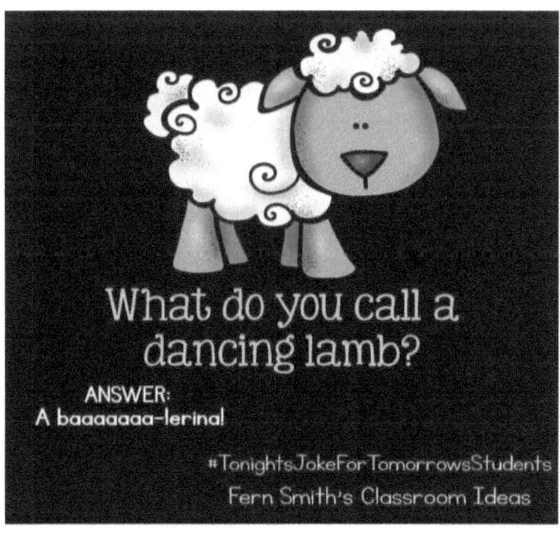

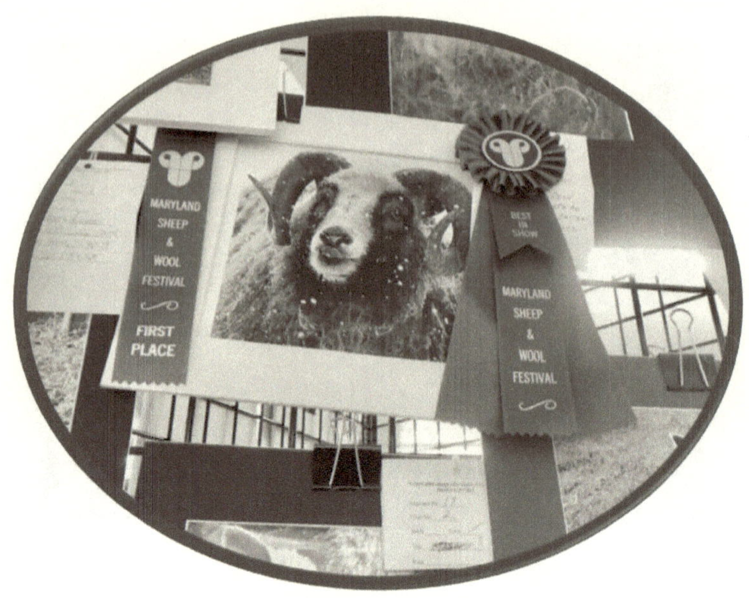

Sheila The Sheep Series include:

Sheila The Sheep Plays The Bagpipes
Sheila The Sheep Goes To The York Fair
Sheila The Sheep Goes To The Spa
Sheila The Sheep Goes To The Farm Show

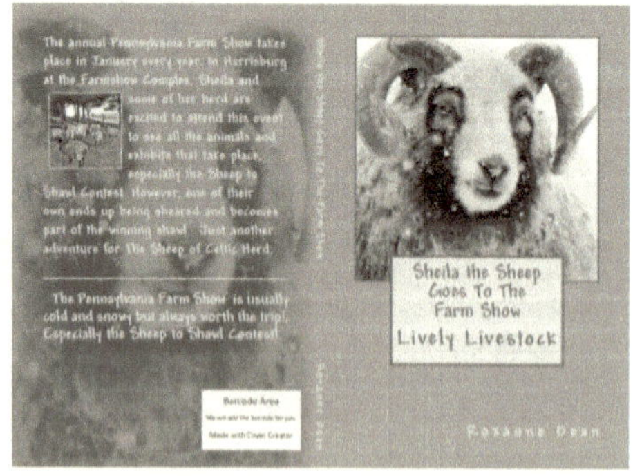

A Book Review by
Nathan Griffith

From time to time *sheep!* has published photos and reports by Roxanne Dean about several southern Pennsylvania wool and sheep activities and also photos of her flock of Scottish Blackface and Shetland sheep.

Now she's published a book of her witty verse about sheep. No, wait—it's about the *people* and the *things* with which the sheep interact: The poems and short stories are written from the point of view as if the sheep were doing the rhyming.

I personally found this book hilarious as I read its witty and "down home style" poems. Its abundant sprinkling of "slant rhyme" amid true rhyme and frequently broken-up meter amid more exact rhythm are aspects that in this book only add to the smiles, chuckles and belly-laughs.

Opportune placement of its peculiar photos, showing funny sheep antics, are also essential, adding to the merriment.

The book is not a long read, a bit over 90 pages and under $10 on Amazon.com.

It's a great stocking stuffer. Or it's an "anytime book," for that special sheep person in your life who seems to already have everything he or she wants.

The title just came out on August 9, 2014, so one thing is certain—they won't yet have this book!

November/December 2014

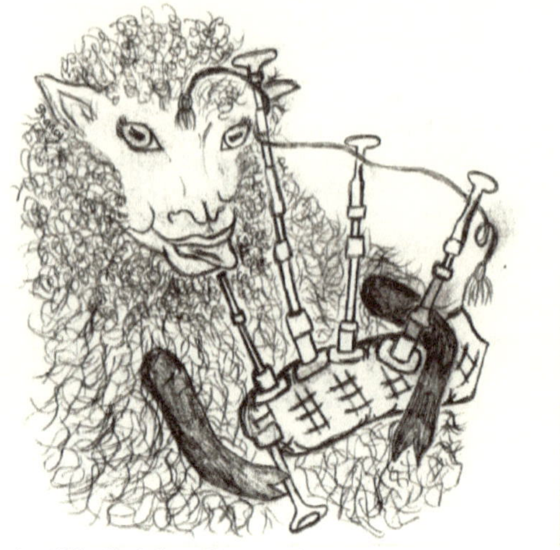

From Book: "Sheila The Sheep Plays The Bagpipes"

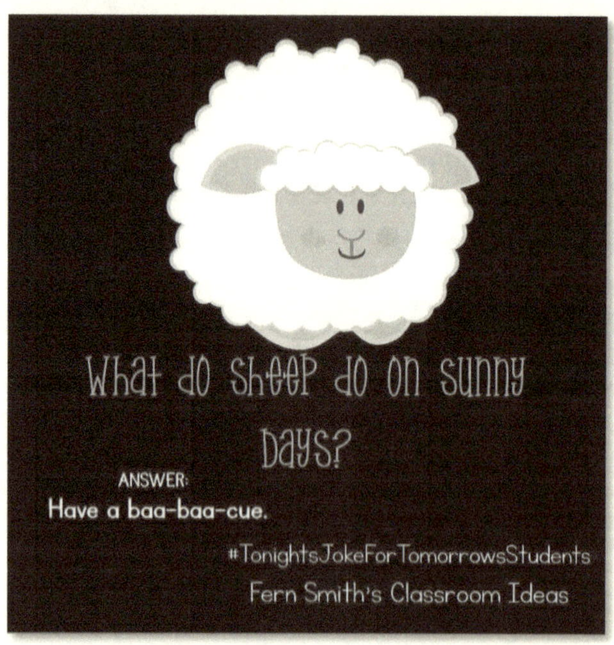

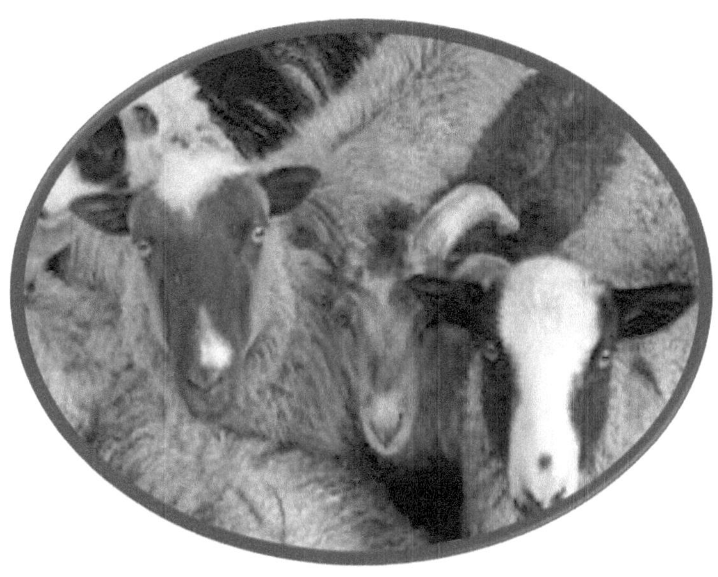

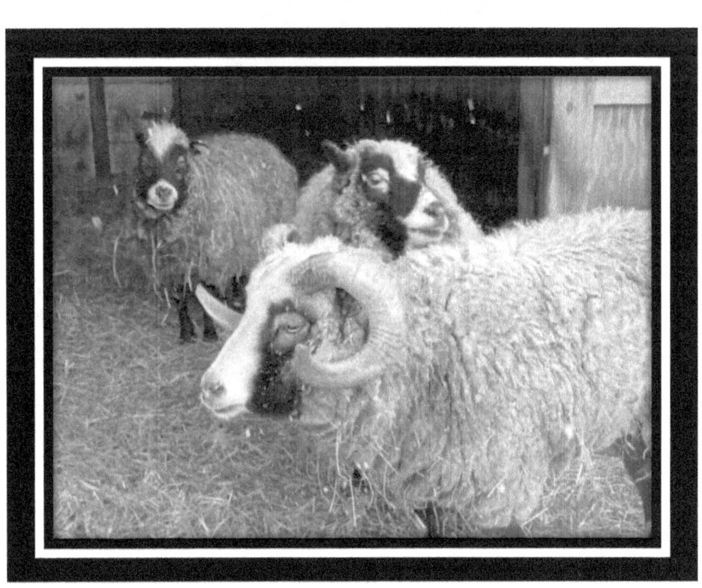

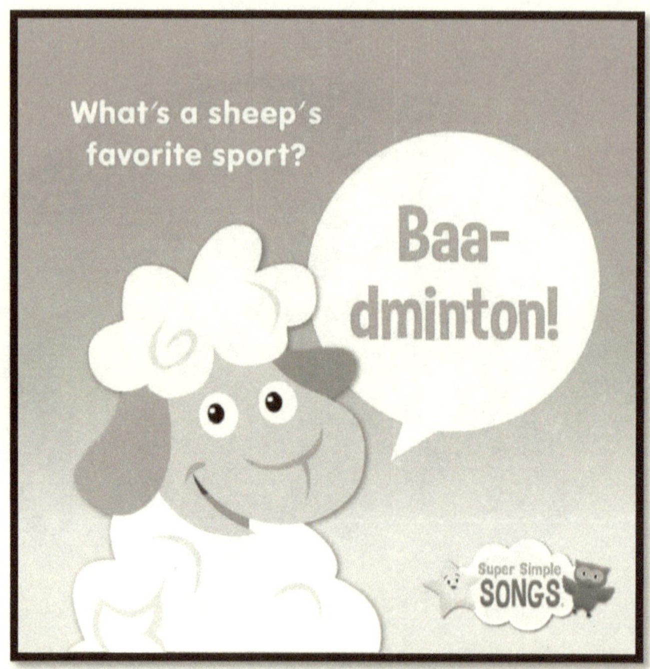

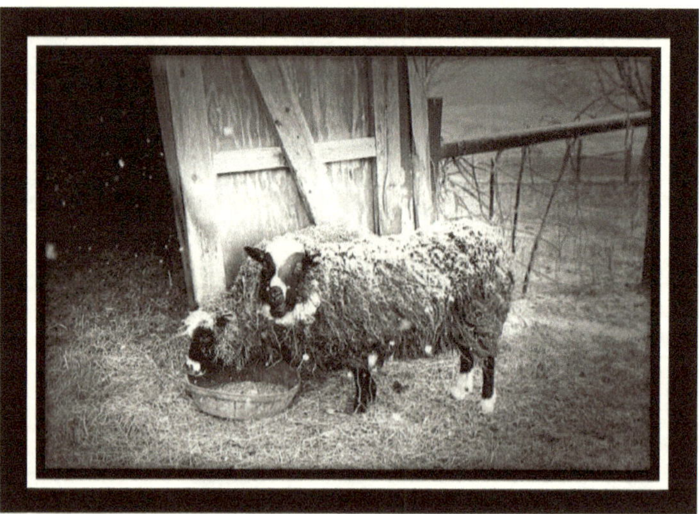

Shetlands in Snow

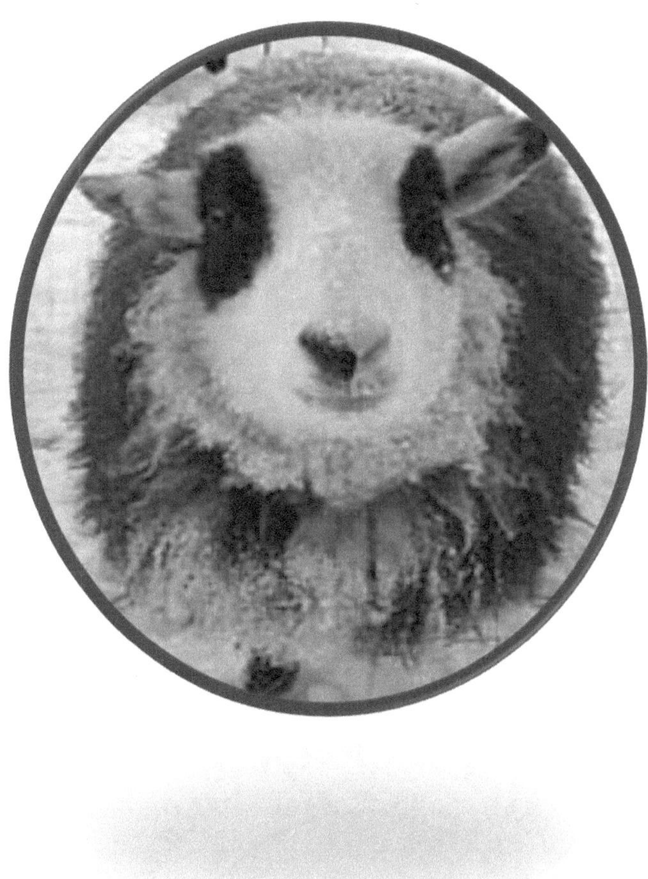

Yuglet Shetland

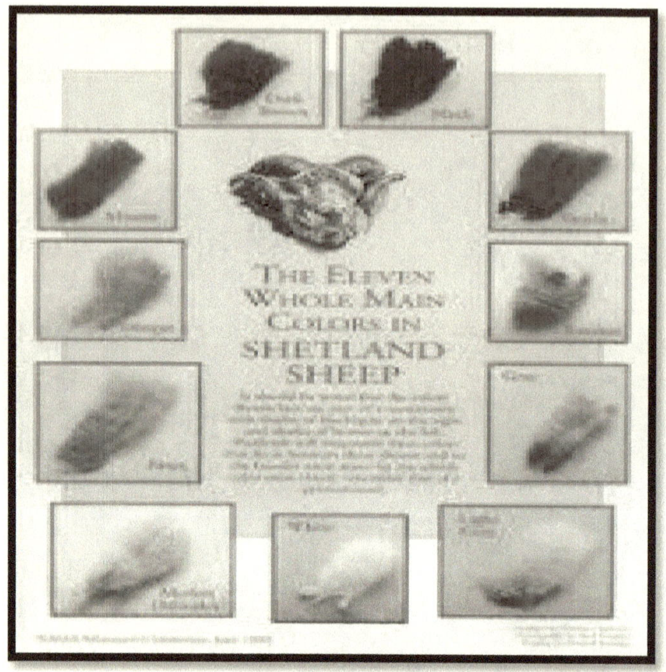

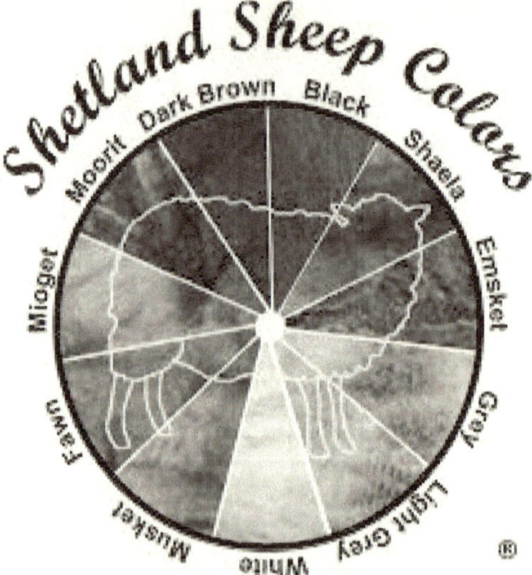

North American Shetland Sheep Association

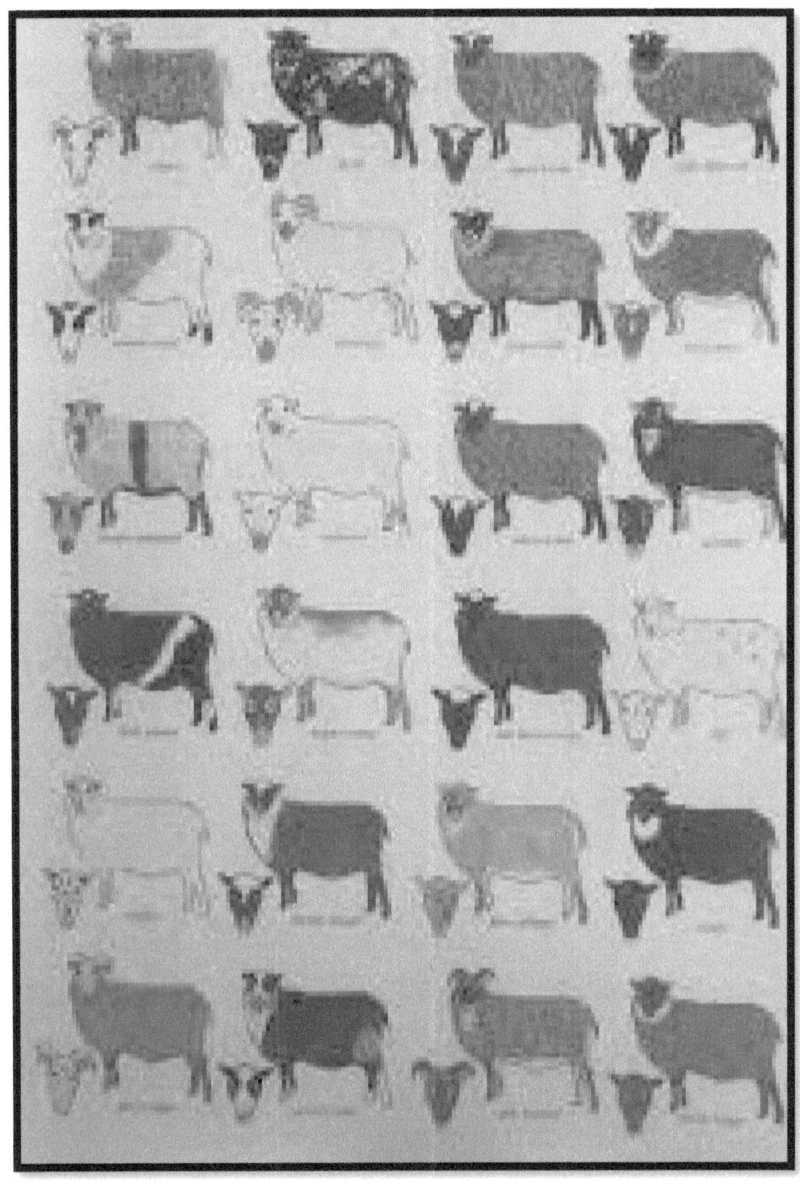

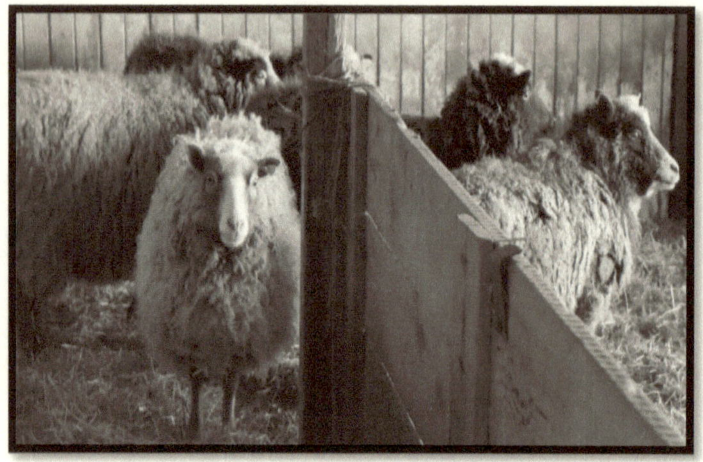

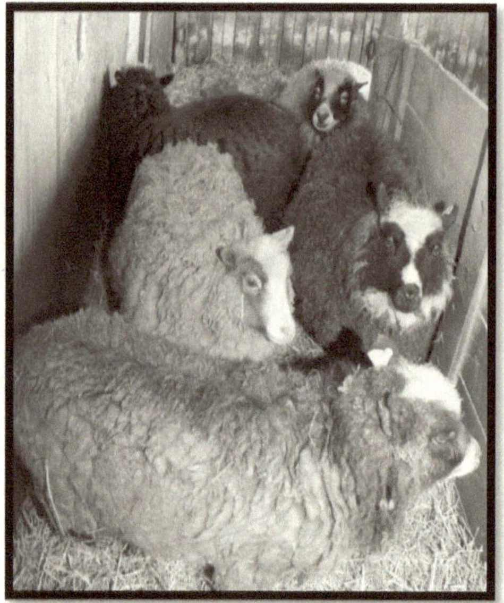

Shetland Markings

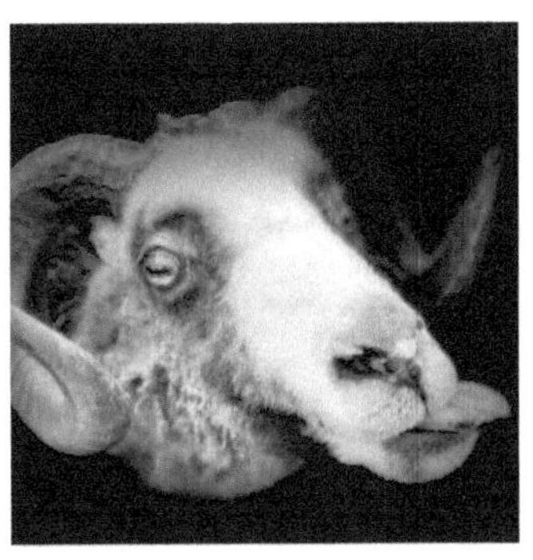

Images of Sheep in Disney Movies

bing.com/images

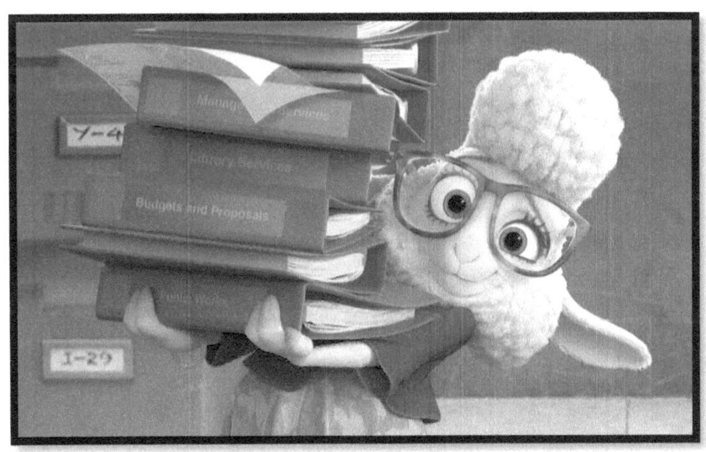

Zootopia

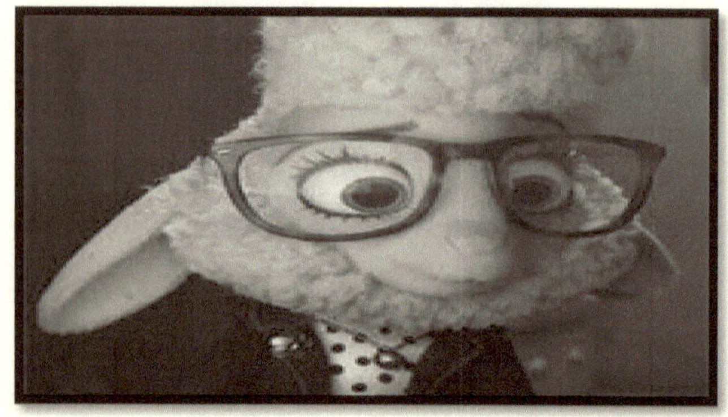

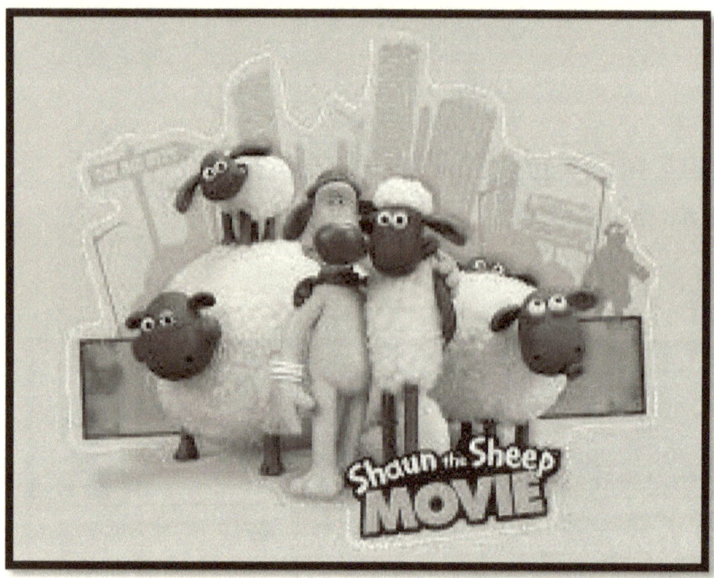

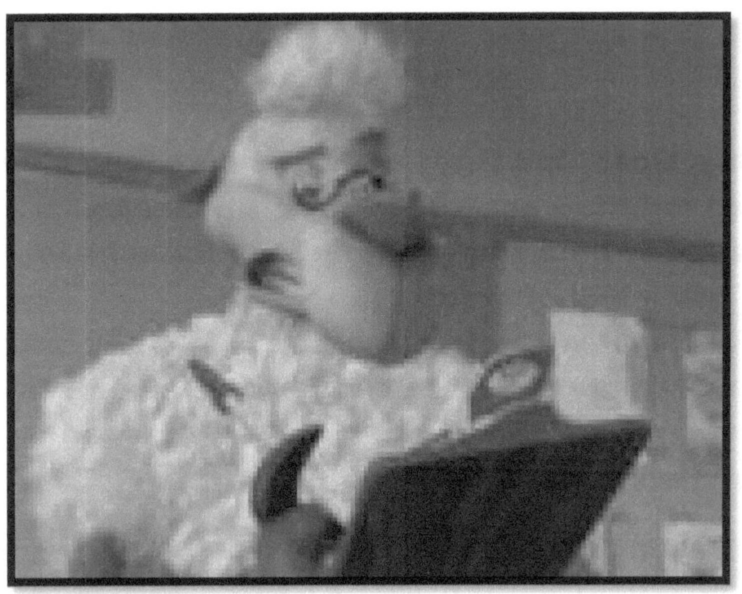

Mr. Woolensworth is a supporting character in Disney's 2005 animated feature film, *Chicken Little*.
He is the schoolteacher of Chicken Little himself at least in one class.

Billy, Goat, and Gruff are three porcelain sheep joined together and sometimes mistakenly believed to be a single sheep with three heads who are minor characters in the Disney/Pixar *Toy Story* franchise. They are always wandering off and enjoy causing mischief and when they do, they can only be stopped by their shepherdess, Bo Peep.

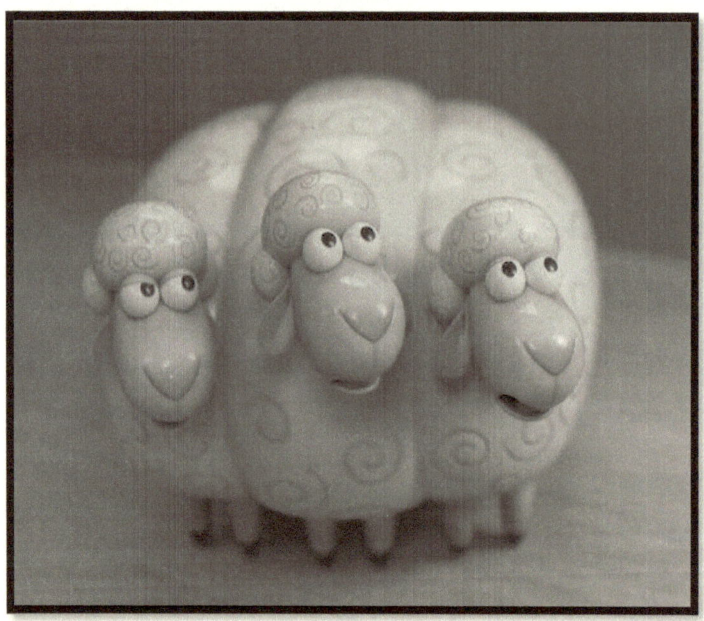

Lambie is one of the main characters from the 2012 Disney Junior series *Doc McStuffins*.

45

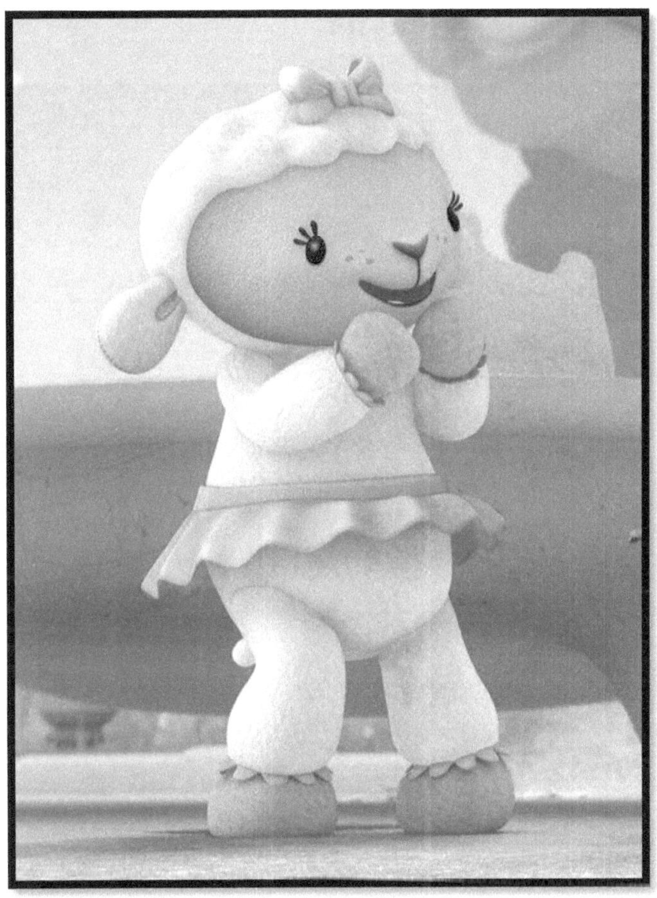

Woolter and Jesse are two minor antagonists from Disney's 2016 animated feature film *Zootopia*. They were some of Bellwether's minions.

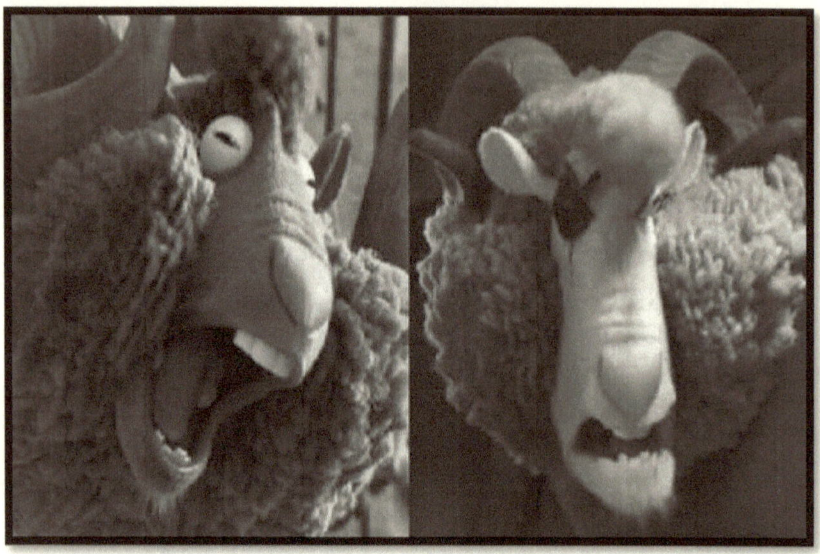

Mrs. Sheep is a character in the 1952 cartoon short *Lambert the Sheepish Lion*. She is the foster mother of the main character, Lambert Lion.

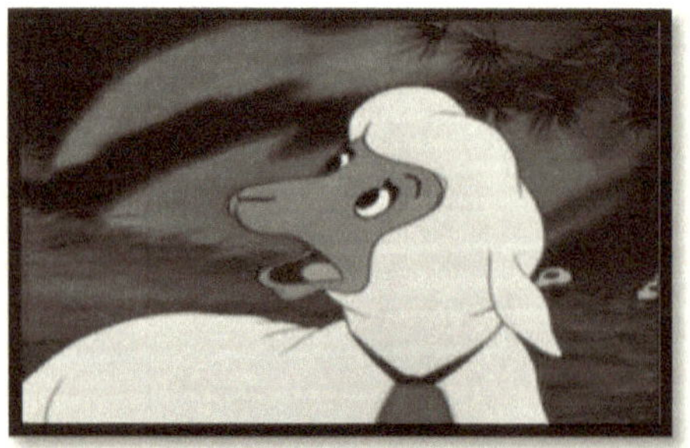

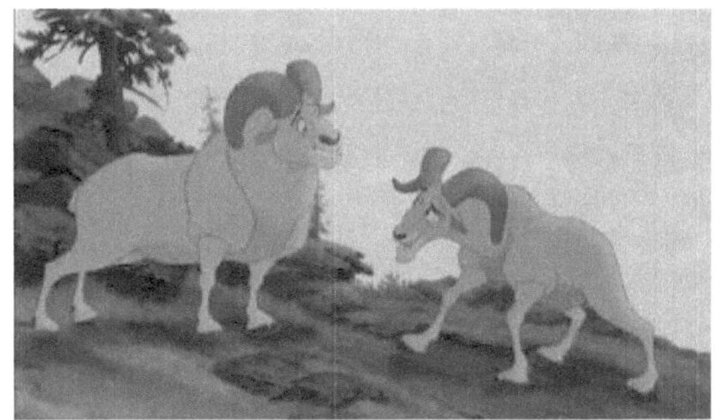

The Rams

**The Rams are some of the characters in :
Brother Bear**

**Sheera is a baby lamb introduced in the
episode Sheer Madness**

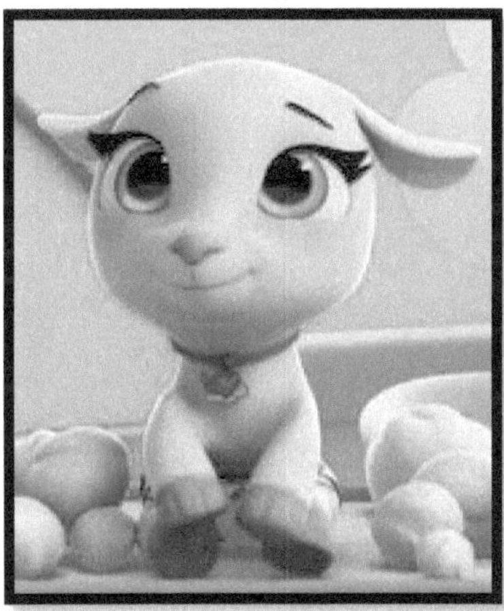

Blackie is a small, black sheep guarded by Pluto in the 1945 animation of *The Legend of Coyote Rock*. She also appeared in 1949's *Sheep Dog*.

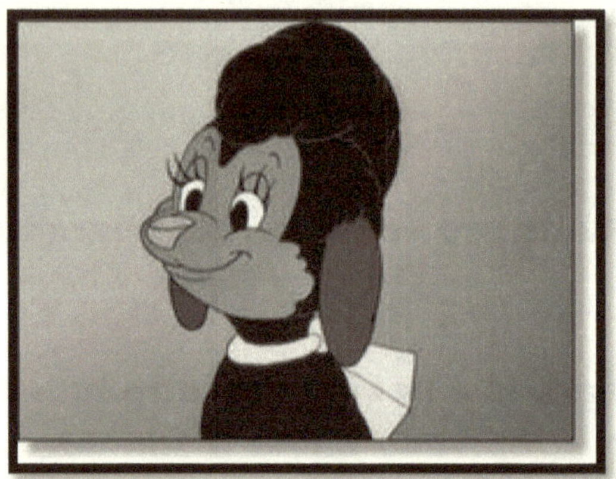

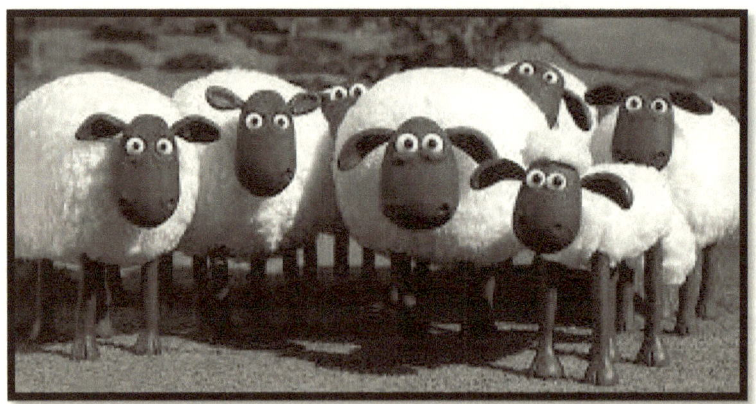

Shaun The Sheep Movie Sheep

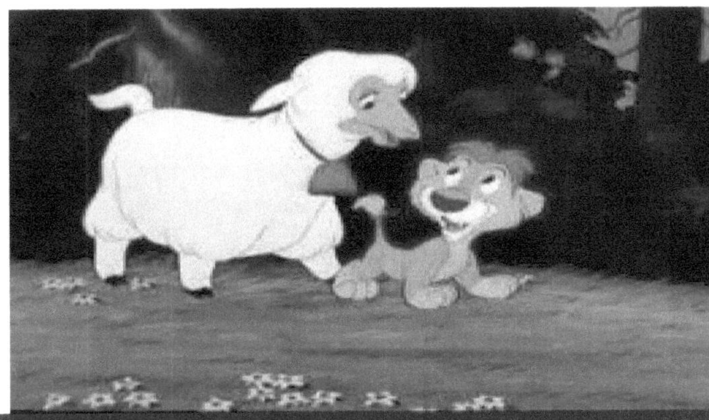

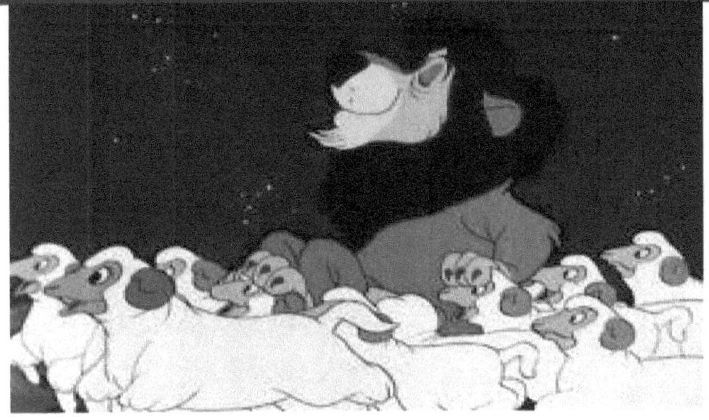

The herd instinct among forecasters makes sheep look like independent thinkers..
-- Edgar Fiedler

<u>It would be equally reasonable to say that sheep are born carnivorous, and everywhere nibble grass.</u>
-- **Emile Faguet**

5. Celtic Herd Characters

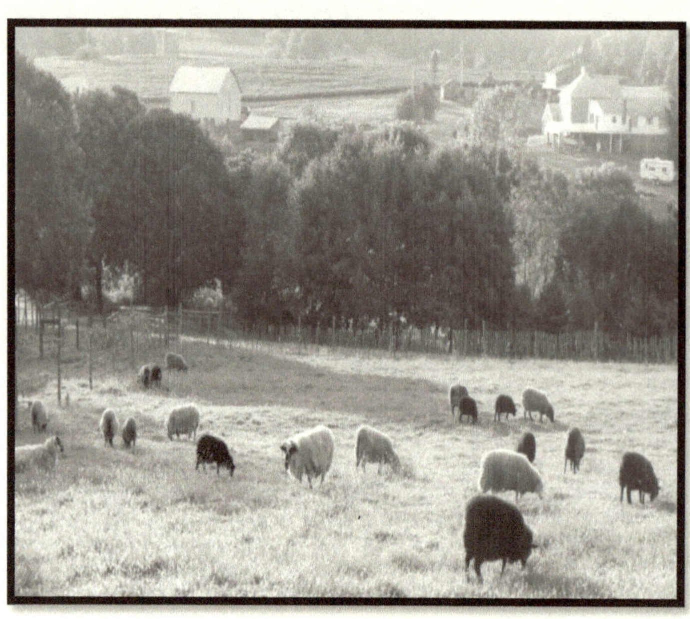

Celtic Herd Sheep/Shetlands and Scottish Blackface

<u>They say beauty is in the eye of the beholder, but us sheep know, true beauty is not in the eye: it lives in the mind.</u>
-- **Craig Stone**.

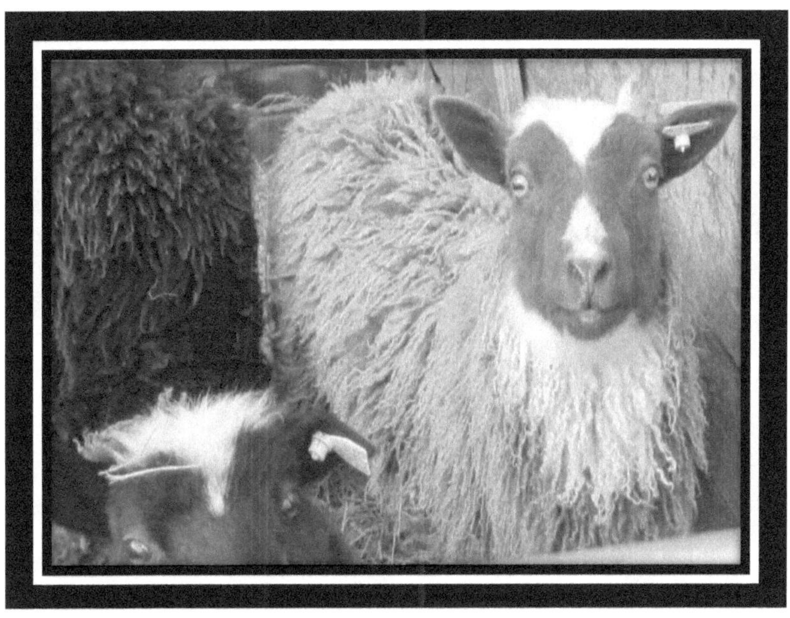

Shetland Ewe Lambs

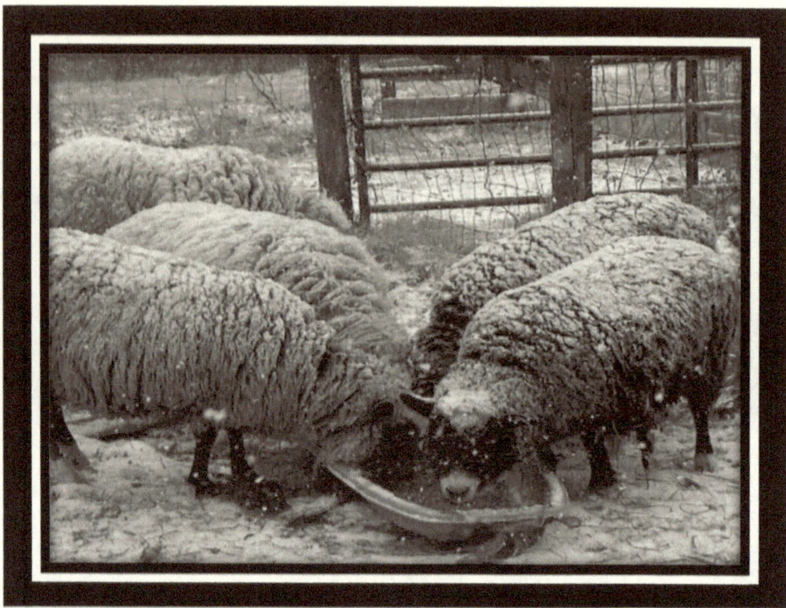

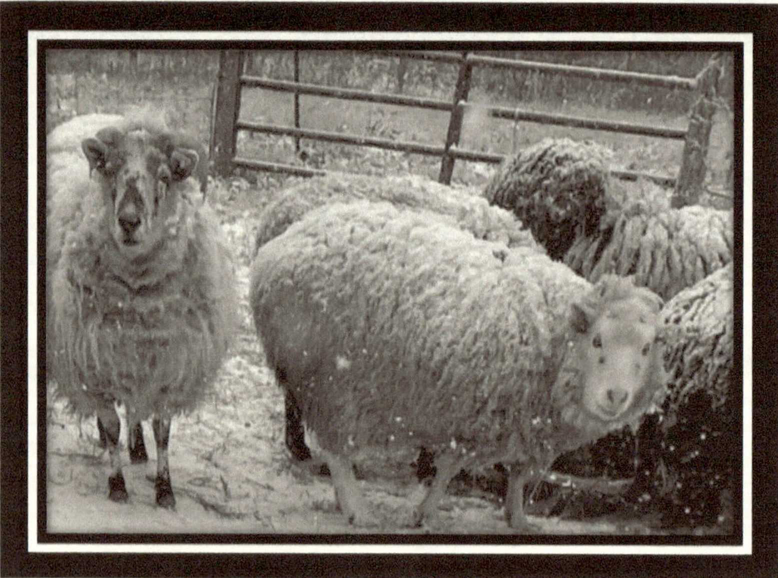

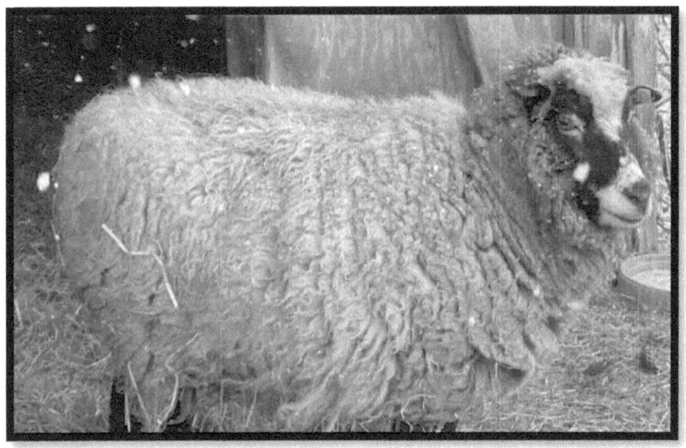

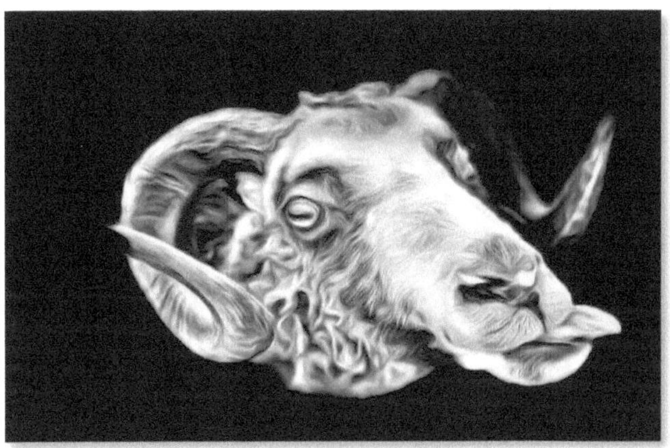

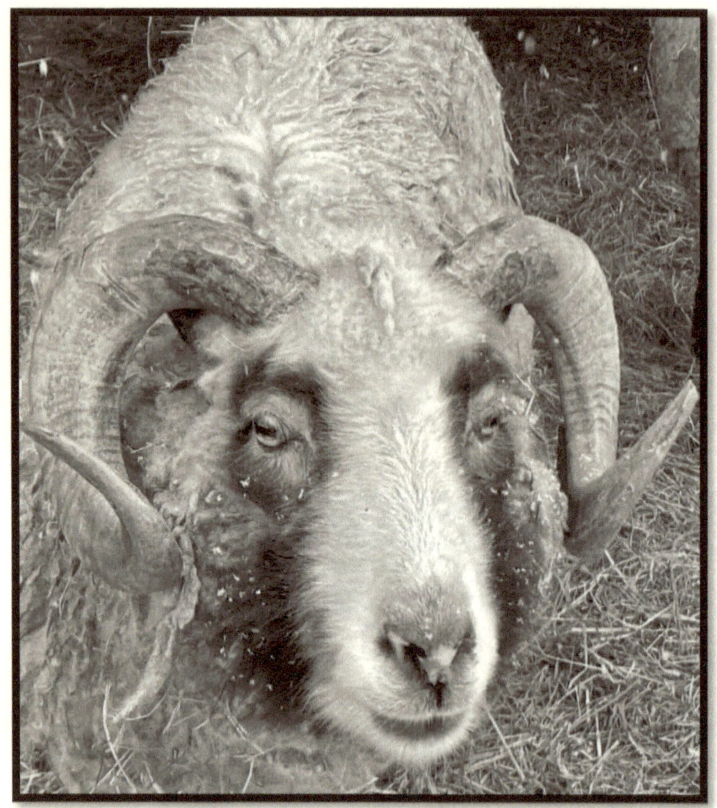

Shetland Ram "Lagavulin"

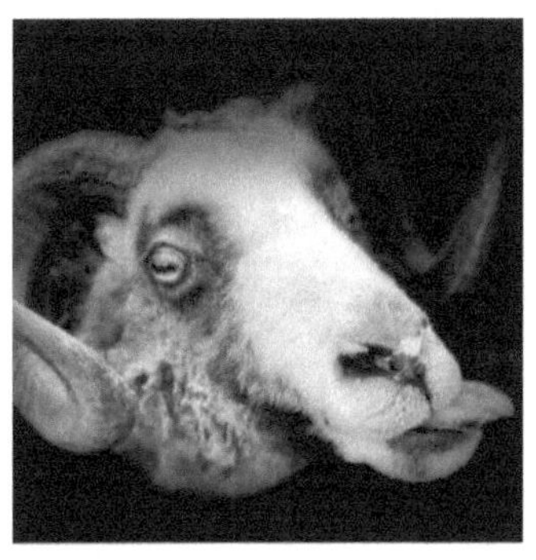

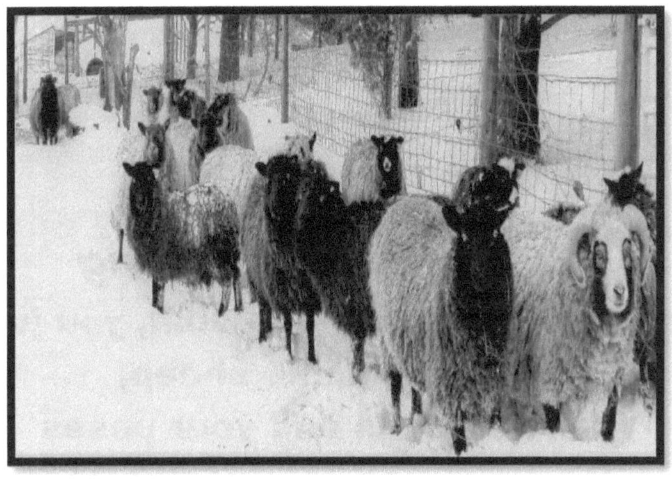

Shetland Sheep are hardy and love the winter snow! They have nice soft fleeces which are perfect for stockings, sweaters and scarves. They are all natural colors Ewes do not have horns like the Scottish blackface ewes do. Mixed breed ewes do have horns.

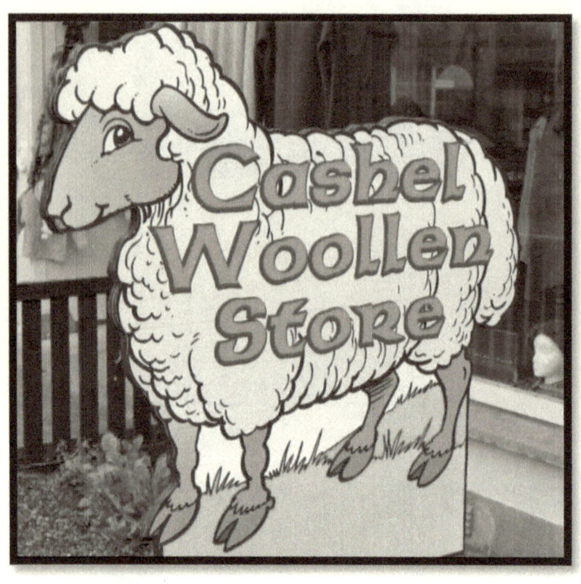

Shop in Ireland by R.Dean

The Shetland's Song

Your faces are un-ewe-usual, you just
don't seem like sheep,
Your markings and your poses
Do make you so ewe-nique!
That fluff ewe walk around with,
So thick and oh so full,
Its color and its texture tells us that it's
your wool!
Some sheep breeds have horns, but
Shetland ewes do not.
Some are just hybrids with colors that

you got.
Why are some of you white and others
shades of gray?
It's all in your heritage, your breed DNA!
Shetlands your tails are fluked - 4-5
inches in all.
When you run, they flop up and down
Your energy is in awe!
You're never in a hurry, if no one is
around.
You sit and chew all day long,
This tune is the Shetland's Song!

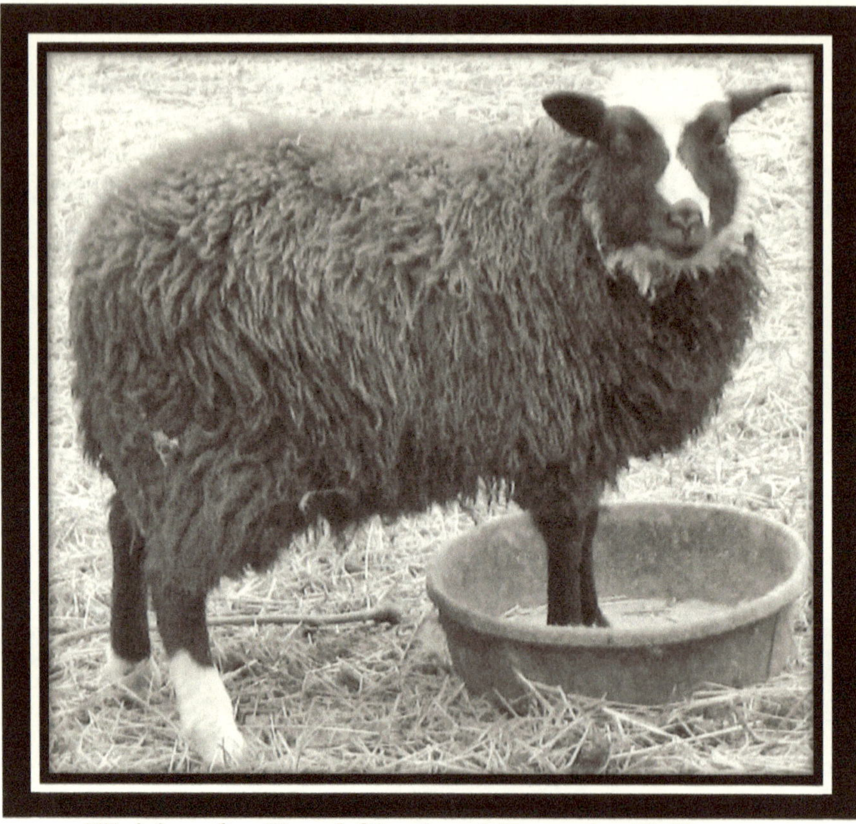

Waiting for Food Shetland Ewe- by R.Dean

I'll stand in my food bowl until you decide to fill it.
I am waiting patiently for you to bring my meal
And I won't move till you do it!
I need my feed so I can grow, I am only a little lamb.
Bring something good that I can chew or this is where
I stand!!!

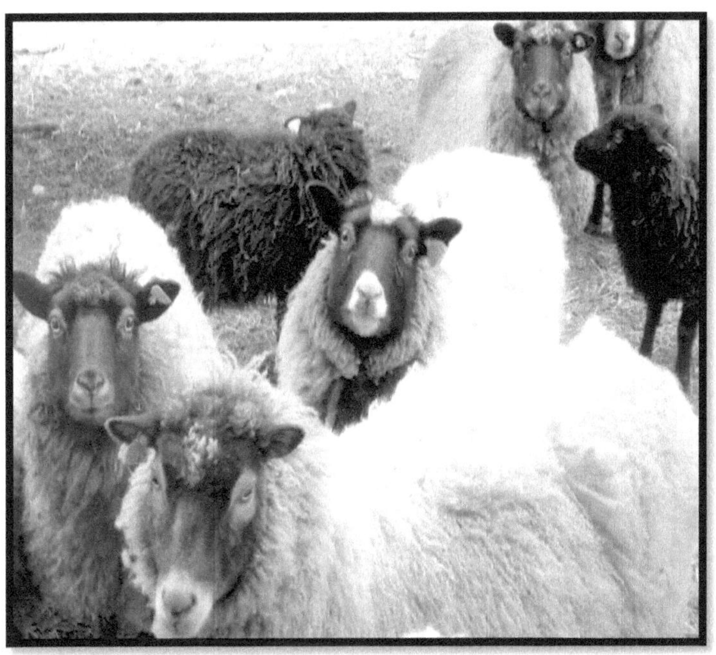

Shetland Faces! By R.Dean

We have different color faces and different color noses. The circles around our eyes help you to see our poses.
Our fleeces can have two colors and sometimes we have a mane. Regardless how you view us we are basically the same.

<u>New Zealand is a country of thirty thousand million sheep, three million of whom think they are human.</u>
-- **Barry Humphries**t

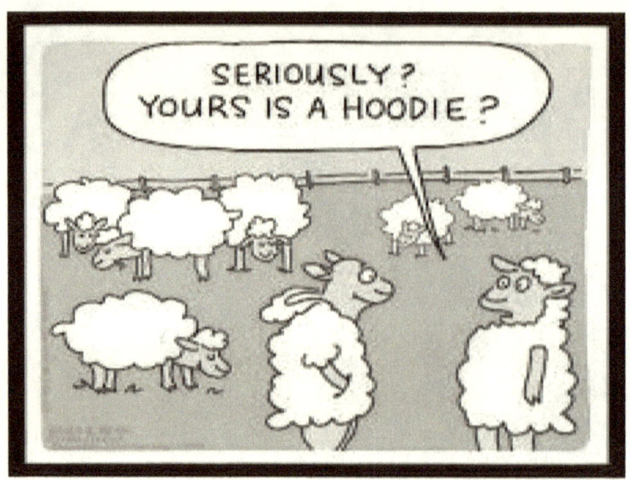

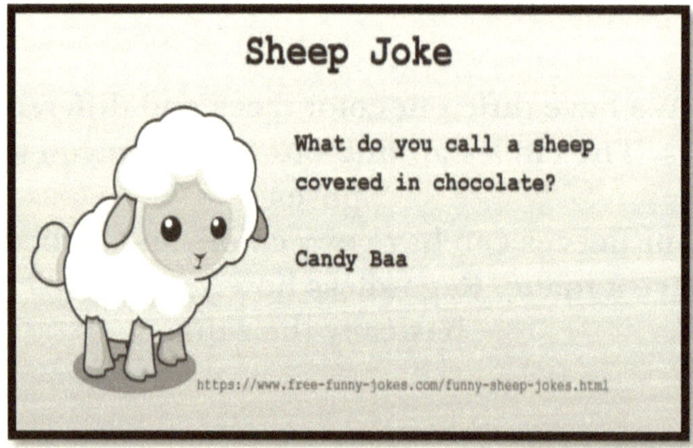

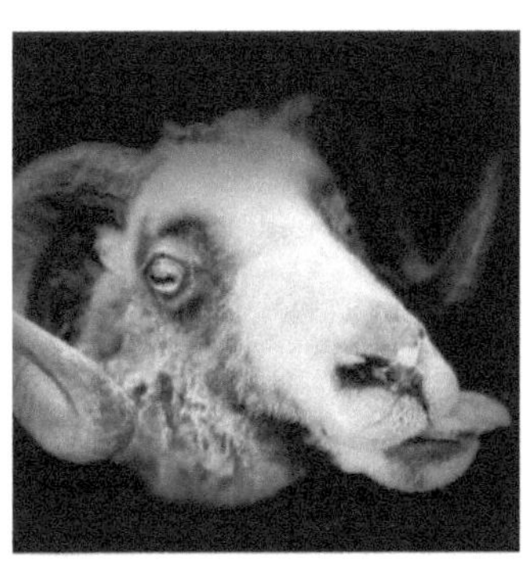

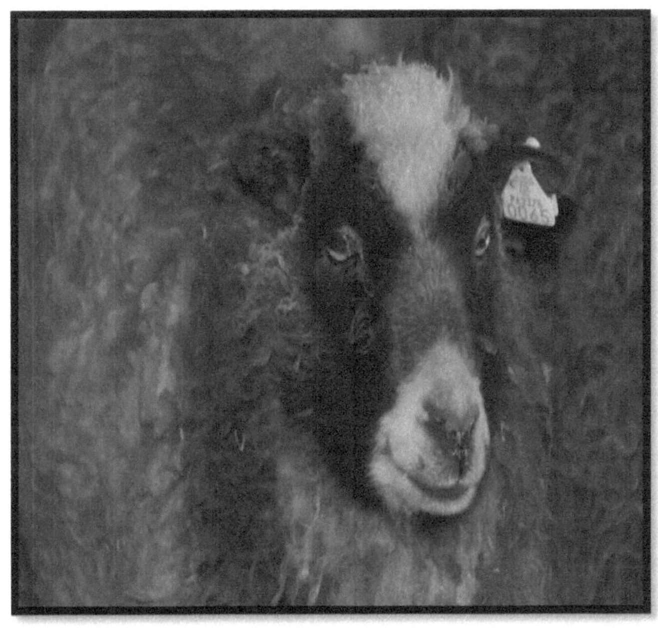

Shetland Ewe- Celtic Herd

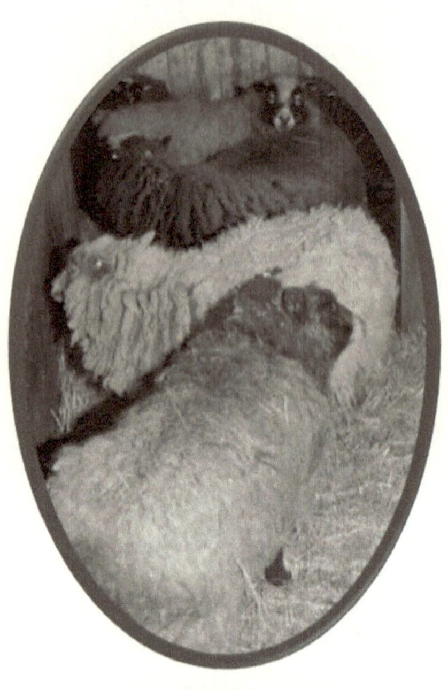

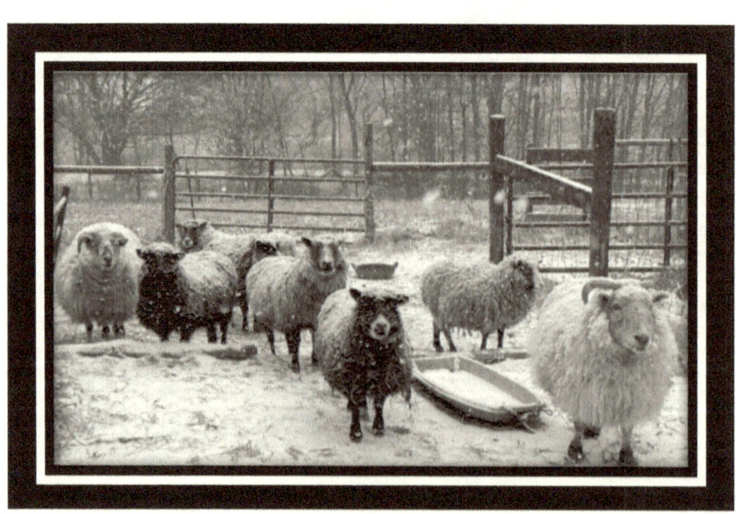

6. 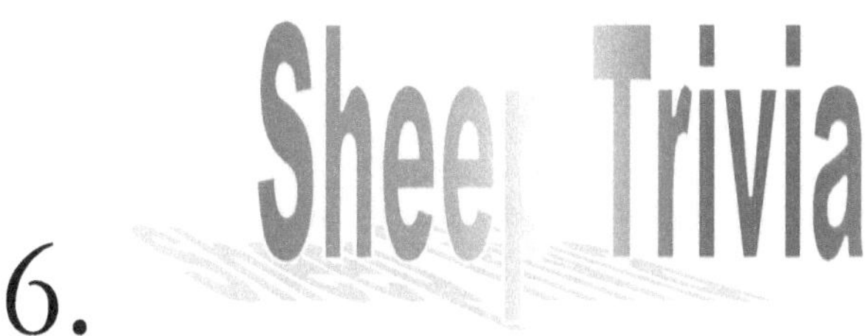

Free Easy Sheep Trivia!

How many domestic sheep are there in the world?
A: Over one billion.

What is an adult female sheep called?
A: A ewe.

What is a non-castrated male called?
A: A ram.

What is a castrated male called?
A: A wether.

What is a younger sheep called?
A: A lamb.

Sheep are most likely descended from what?
A: The wild mouflon of Europe and Asia.

One of the earliest animals to be domesticated for agricultural purposes, sheep are raised for what?
A: Fleece, meat (lamb, hogget or mutton) and milk.

A sheep's wool is the most widely used what?
A: Animal fiber

Wool is usually harvested by what method?
A: Shearing

Ovine meat is called "what" when from younger animals?
A: Lamb.

What is it called when it comes from older animals?
A: Mutton.

Sheep continue to be important for wool and meat today, and are also occasionally raised for what?
A: Pelts, as dairy animals, or as model organisms for science.

Sheep husbandry is practiced throughout the majority of the what?
A: Inhabited world.

In the modern era, what areas are most closely associated with sheep production?
A: Australia, New Zealand, the southern and central South American nations, and the British Isles are.

What is a group of sheep called?
A: A flock, herd or mob.

In both ancient and modern religious ritual, sheep are used as what?
A: Sacrificial animals

Colors of domestic sheep range from pure white to what?
A: Dark chocolate brown, and even spotted or piebald.

"What" began early in sheep domestication?
A: Easily dyeable white fleeces.

Because white wool is a dominant trait it did what?
A: Spread quickly.

White wool is desirable for large commercial markets, there is a "what" for colored fleeces?
A: Niche market, mostly for hand spinning.

The nature of the fleece varies widely among the breeds, from dense and highly crimped, to what?
A: Long and hair-like.

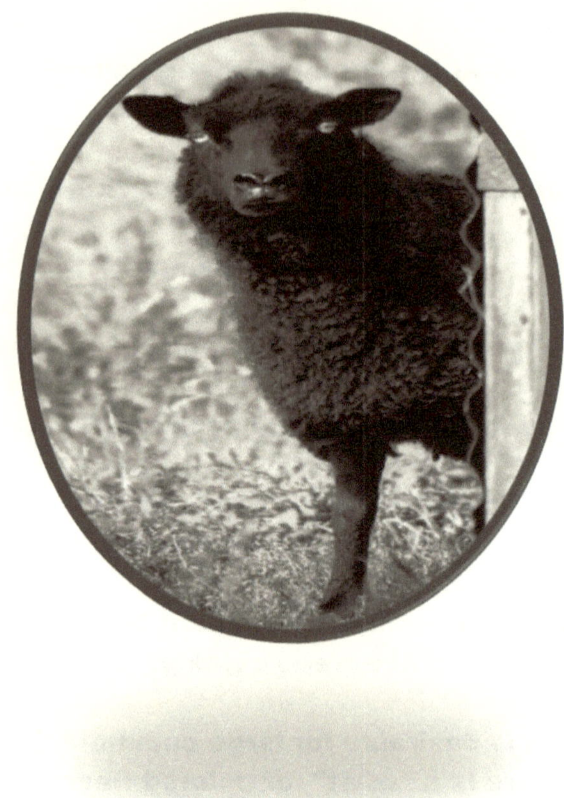

**Sheila The Shetland Ewe:
Photo by Susan Keller**

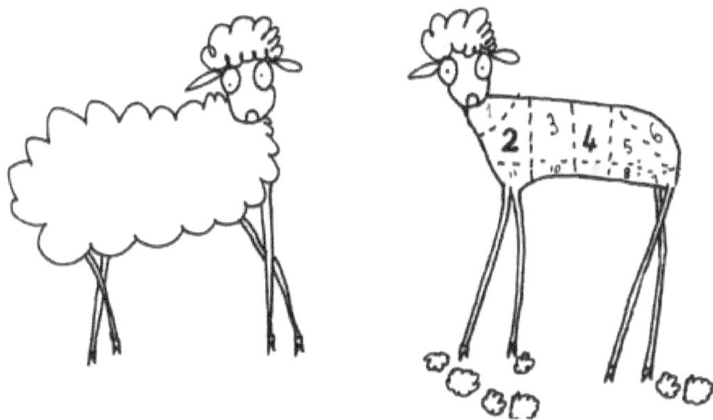

In the U.S. Texas, Wyoming and California have the highest number of sheep. More sheep are in the Southern Plains, and The Mountain and Pacific regions.

Products made from sheep include: tennis rackets with strings made of sheep guts
Candles and soap made of tallow rendered from sheep fat.
Skincare products use lanolin, an emollient found in sheep's wool.
 Sheep can recognize up to 50 other sheep faces and remember them for 2 years. They can also recognize human faces.

Wool cloth existed as far back as 10,000 B.C. By the time the Romans invaded Britain in 55 B.C. The wool industry had already been developed in the nation.

Sheep's milk is ideal for making cheese. It contains higher levels of calcium, vitamins A, B and E and other nutritional elements than cow's milk. Many types of sheep's milk cheese include: Greek feta, French Roquefort, Spanish manchego, sheep's milk ricotta, and pecorino romano from Italy.

Sheep are known for their peripheral vision. They have rectangular pupils which allow them to see almost 360 degrees which gives them the ability to see behind themselves without turning their heads

Sheep wool is durable, insulating, wrinkle-resisting, fire-resistant and moisture-absorbing. This makes it Ideal for sweaters, coats, rugs, and blankets.

<u>Shrek the Merino sheep</u> hid in a cave for six years so he wouldn't have to get sheared. But the time he was cornered and given his long-overdue haircut on New Zealand national television, there was enough wool to make 20 men's suits.

In 2015, a sheep named <u>Chris</u> who was found in Canberra, Australia, with 89-pounds of fleece.

The wool of domestic breeds like the Merino will just keep growing, according *to Dave Thomas, the now retired head of sheep studies at the University of Wisconsin, Madison.*

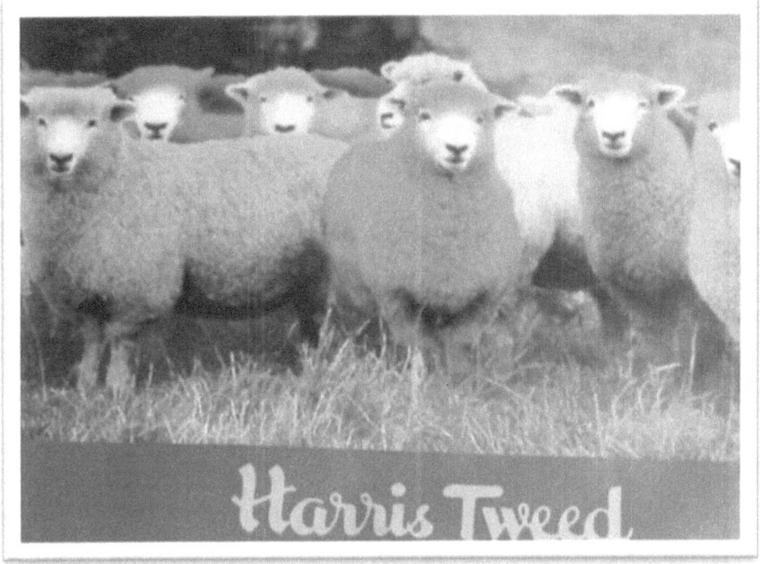

Scottish Blackface Wool is used to make Harris Tweed Jackets!

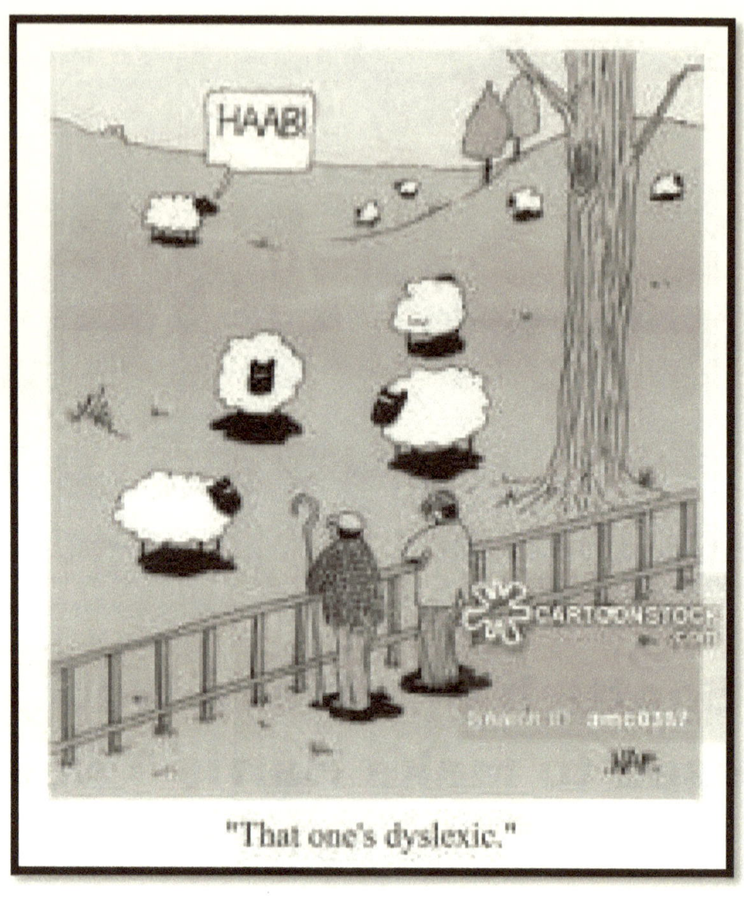

"That one's dyslexic."

7. Just Sheep

Even if sheep could talk, they'd never ask questions.
-- **Andrew Vachss**

Sheep are a prey species, and their only defense is to flee. Flocks include multiple females, offspring, and one or more males. Ewes tend to stay in their maternal groups for life.
Sheep graze in groups.
Flock dynamics are apparent in groups of four or more since they follow a leader or flee in unison.
Even a ewe may charge or threaten by hoof stomping. Separation from the flock can cause stress and panic. Isolation from other sheep can cause severe stress. Sheep respond to food calls, can problem solve,

learn their names, carry packs, and can even be clicker trained.

Sheep have specialized neural mechanisms in the right temporal and frontal lobes of the brain and may recognize familiar human or ovine faces for as long as 2 yr.

SOURCE: https://www.merckvetmanual.com/

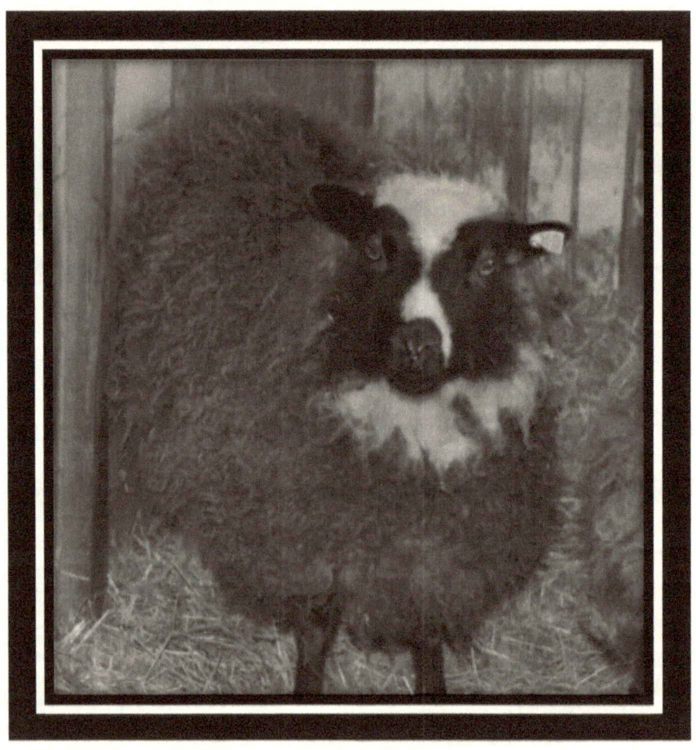

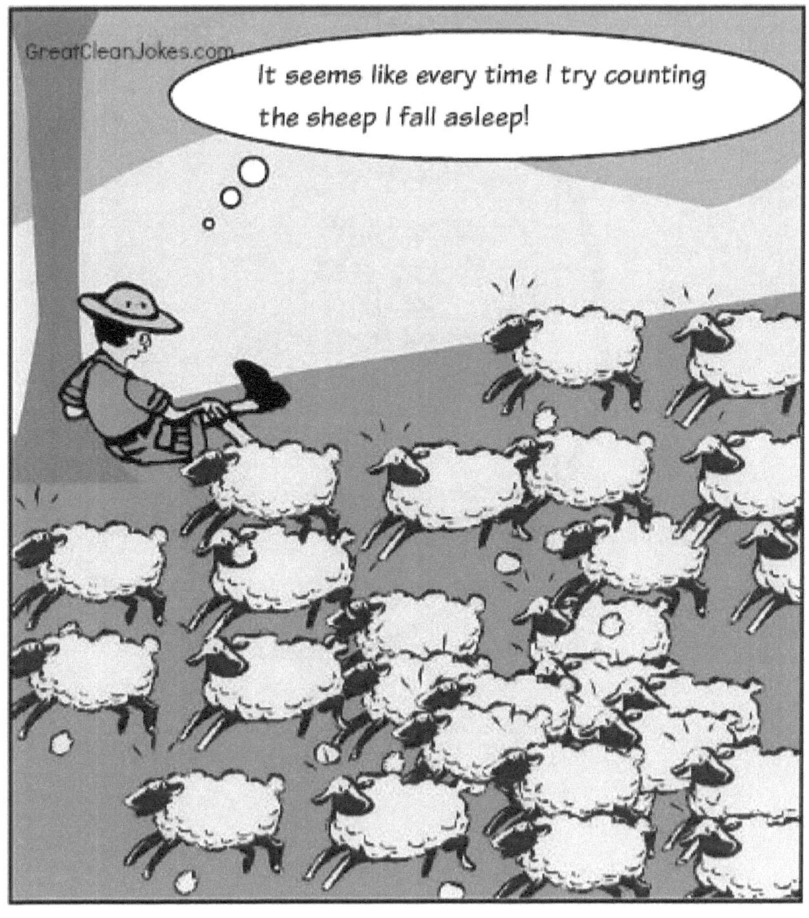
It seems like every time I try counting
the sheep I fall asleep!

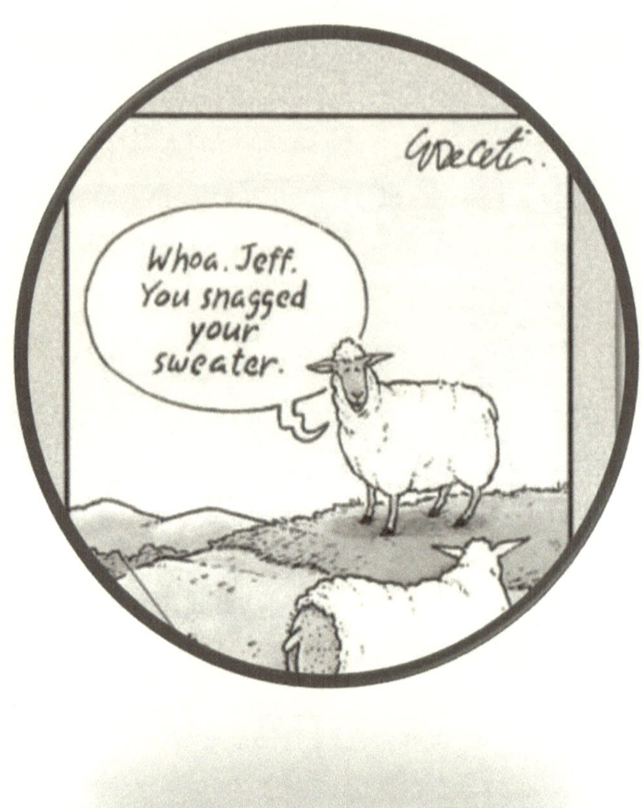

Just Ewe Sheep

**Ewe are ruminants with a special peripheral vision that gives you a 360 degree revision.
Ewe don't have to move to see behind you. Predators don't get an advantage to sneak up unseen, ewe will bolt before**

they're close enough to where you have
been!
Ewe have four stomachs and that's a
fact. Ewe can chew your cud all day and
not get too fat,
Your wool gets to be thick and needs to
be sheared.
If it doesn't ewe will scratch it off and
ruin the crimp –that would ruin its wear!
Ewe can munch in the fields or stay
close to the hay.
Ewe will stay out in the fields and enjoy
the day.
Ewe are actually smart and can
remember human faces.
In fact, ewe stay close to your herd and
their regular places.
Ewe shouldn't be separated at all from
your group, That is dangerous to your
ego, ewe need to stay in your loop.
The herding instinct is important you
see- to follow each other in single file or
to flee!

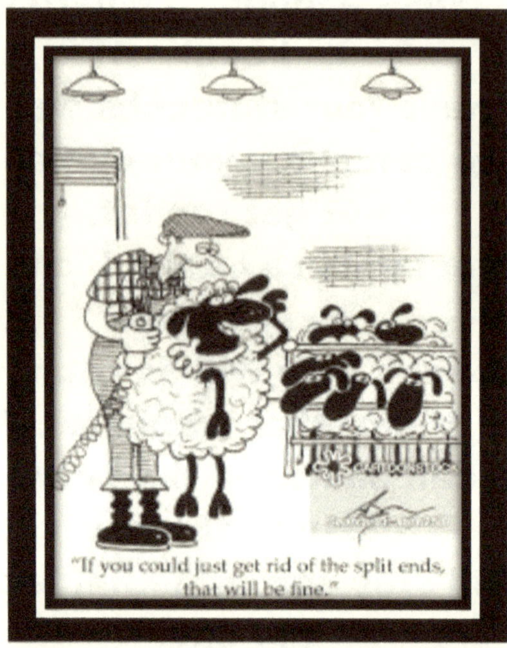

"If you could just get rid of the split ends,
that will be fine."

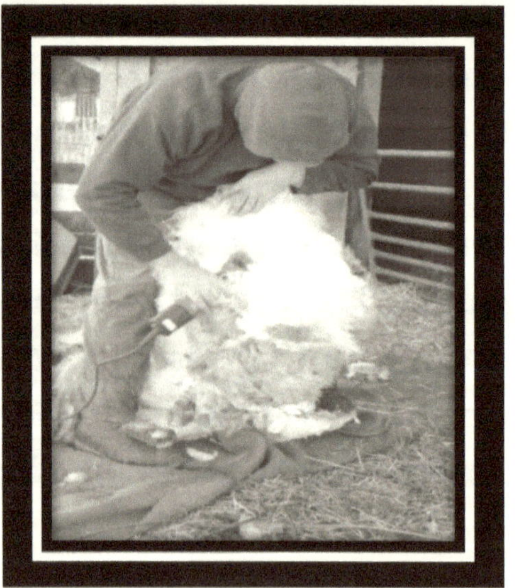

Sheep shearing is the process by which the woolen fleece of a sheep is cut off. The person who removes the sheep's wool is called a shearer. Typically each adult sheep is shorn once each year. Source: Wikipedia

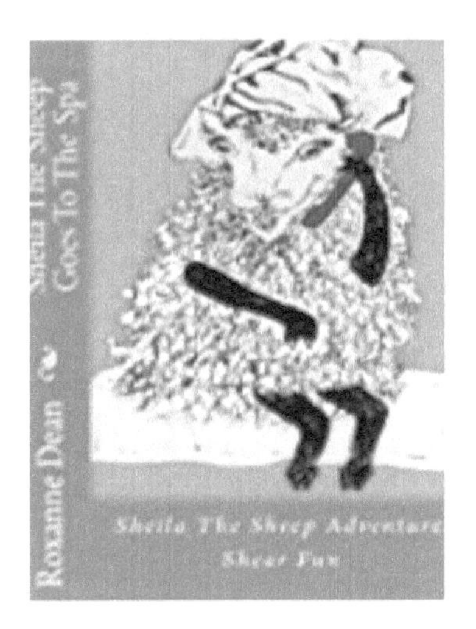

Info on Shearing? Read: "Sheila The Sheep Goes To The Spa"

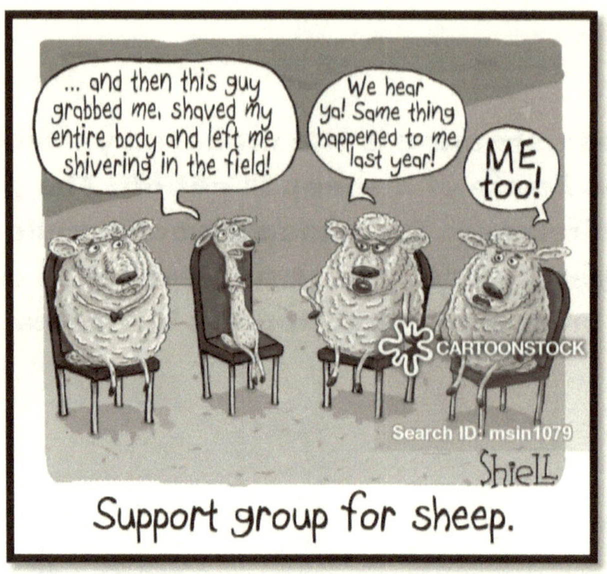

Support group for sheep.

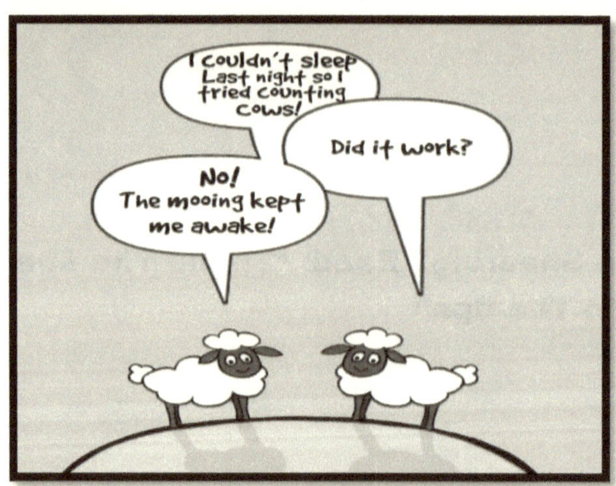

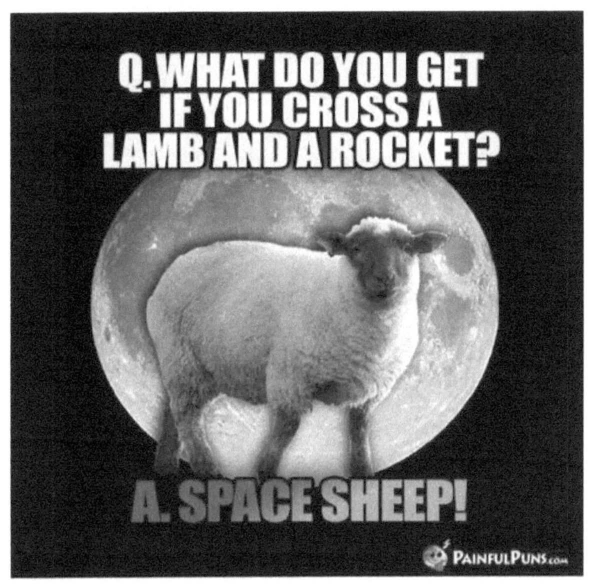
Q. WHAT DO YOU GET
IF YOU CROSS A
LAMB AND A ROCKET?
A. SPACE SHEEP!
PAINFULPUNS.com

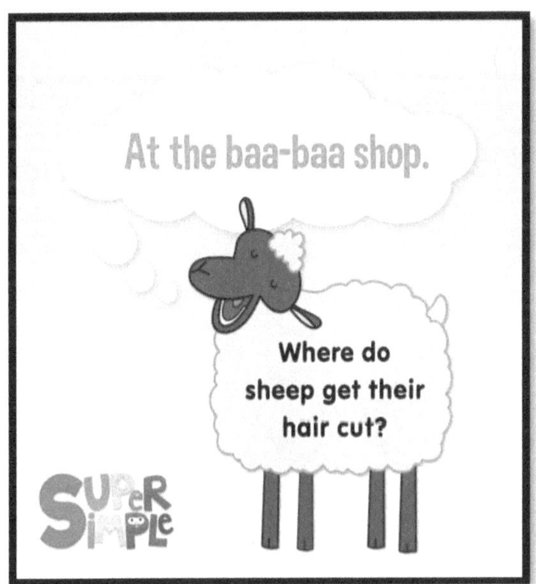
At the baa-baa shop.
Where do
sheep get their
hair cut?
SUPER
SIMPLE

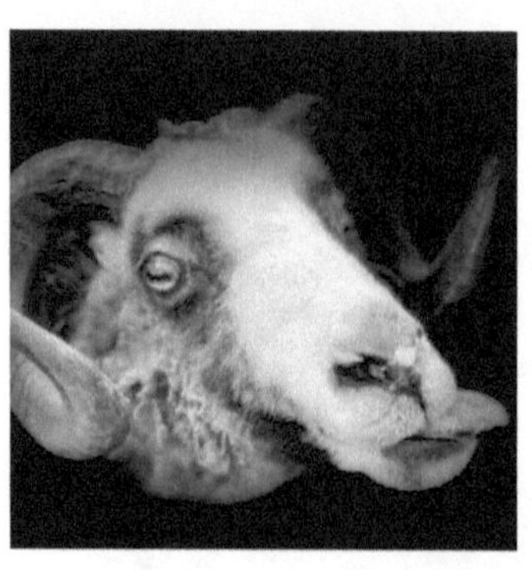

8. Poems and Puns

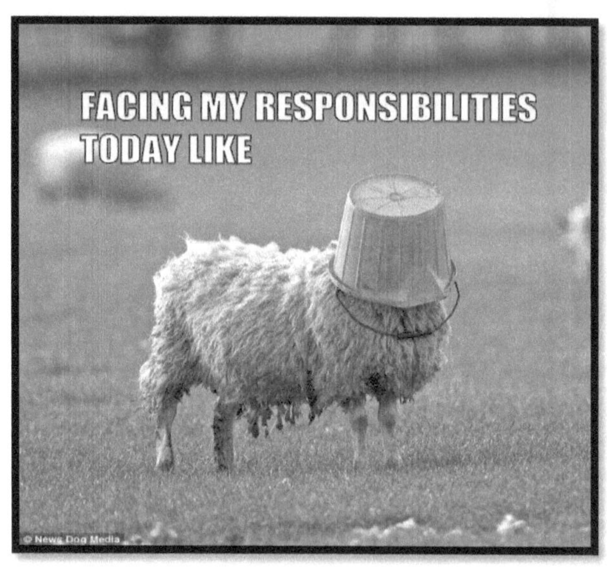

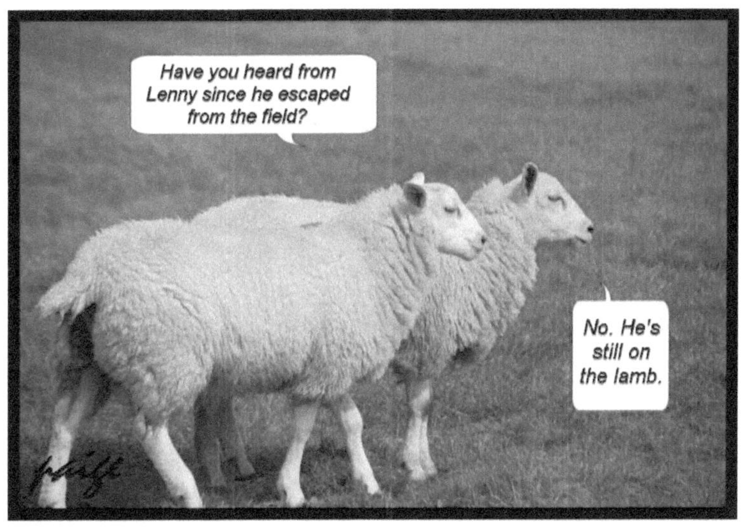

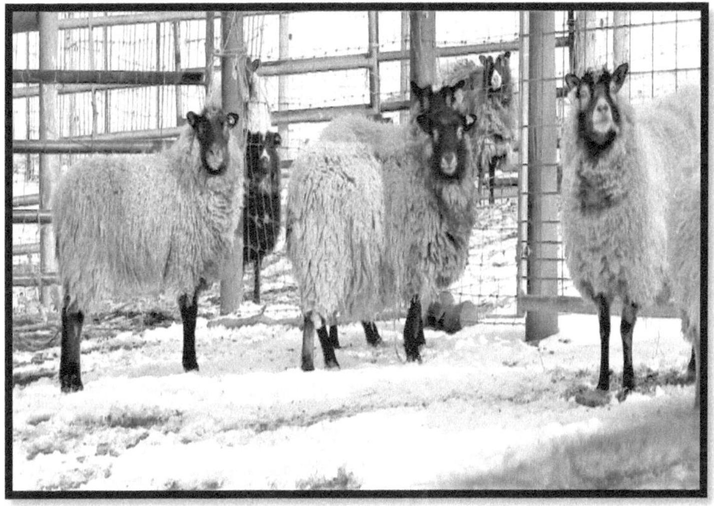

Celtic Herd- Winter by R. Dean

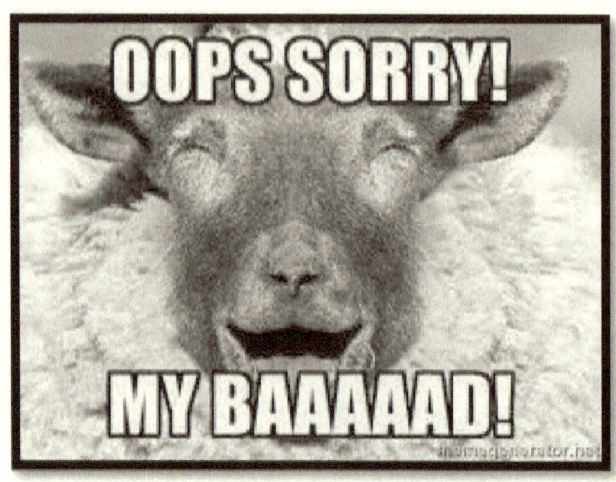

Sheep you are given a baaaaaaaaaaaaaaaad
rap!
People think you are dumb and that's not a
fact.
Ewe are smarter than ewe look but you don't
do a whole lot!
Most of the time you sit and chew and
never seem to stop!
You get up when one of ewe decides to
move. You walk in a straight line behind
whoever is in front of ewe -you might say ewe
have to get in the groove.
It might take awhile to actually get from
point A to point B.
In fact, it can take hours before you end up
following the leader after many stops, ewe
take your time -you are calm and free.
When one of ewe stops so does the herd.
Rambling along without hurrying, it seems
absurd.

**If ewe are spooked, ewe can certainly run
in every direction sometimes for fun!
Entertaining ewe are with your crazy
antics -then you suddenly just stop when
you're no longer frantic.
Ewe seem to smile enjoying the joke and
letting the people see you giving that smirk.
The laugh is on us ewe seem to be saying,
that's okay -we love seeing you playing.**

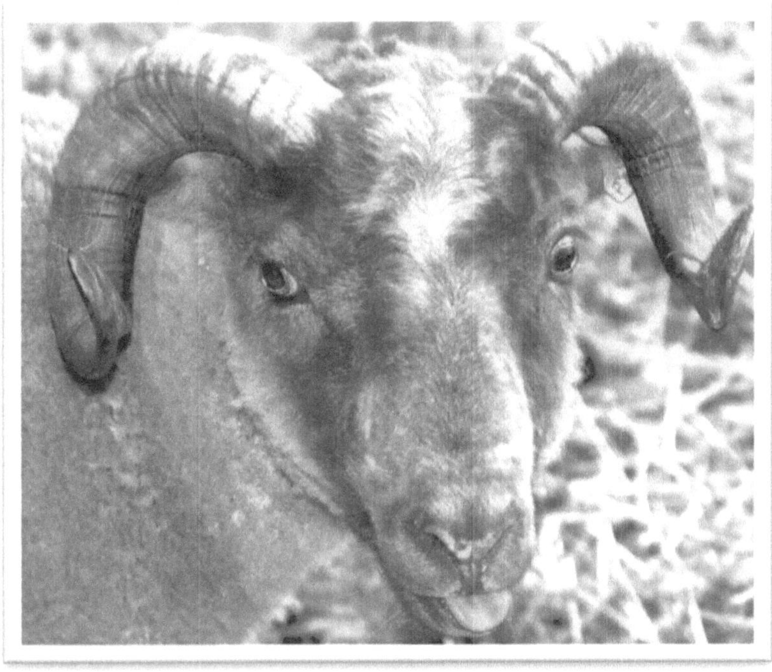

Shetland Ram -Moorit by R.Dean

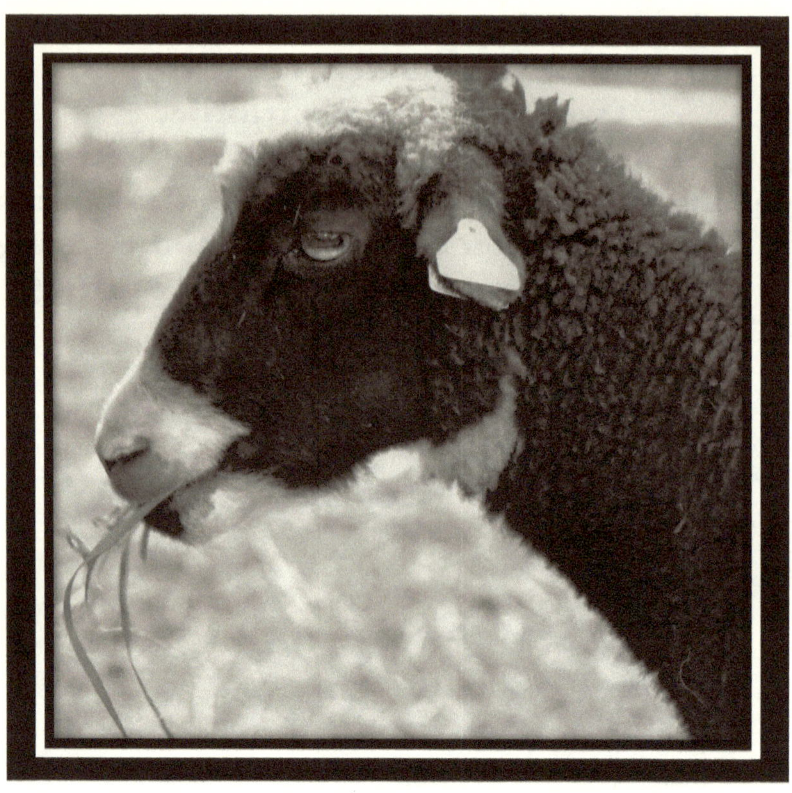

Chewing on Grass -it's part of the day, it is the
first choice to partake and then comes the hay!
Ewe can cut off more than you can chew
because you have talent, that's what you do!
Save it for later, it has lots of flavor-
Clumps at a time, aww ewe can still savor!
Grass has lots of protein, it can vary in taste.
Ewe can try out mouthfuls at a time- don't want
any waste.
Grasses smell yummy when they have a touch

**of some rain. The wetter they are, the better the
strain.
Chewing your cud is better with grass
Ewe don't have to stop chewing
or chew it too fast!**

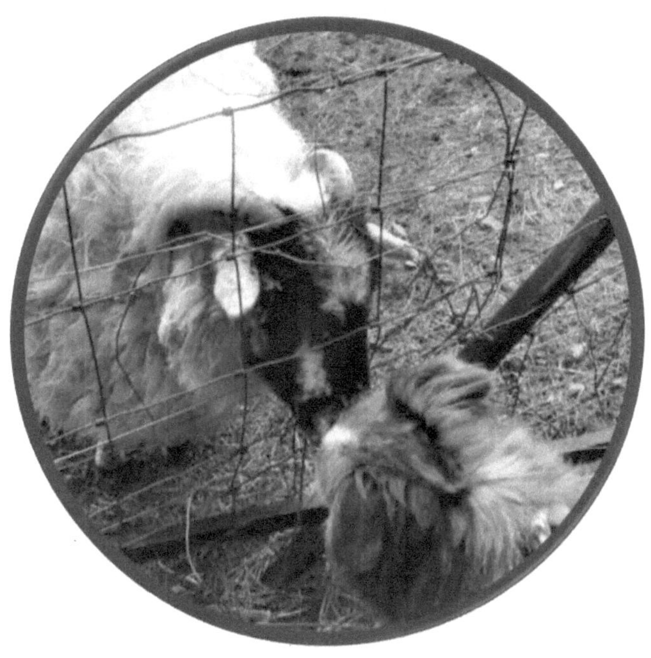

**Scottish Blackface Ewe and Australian
Shepherd Get Acquainted!**

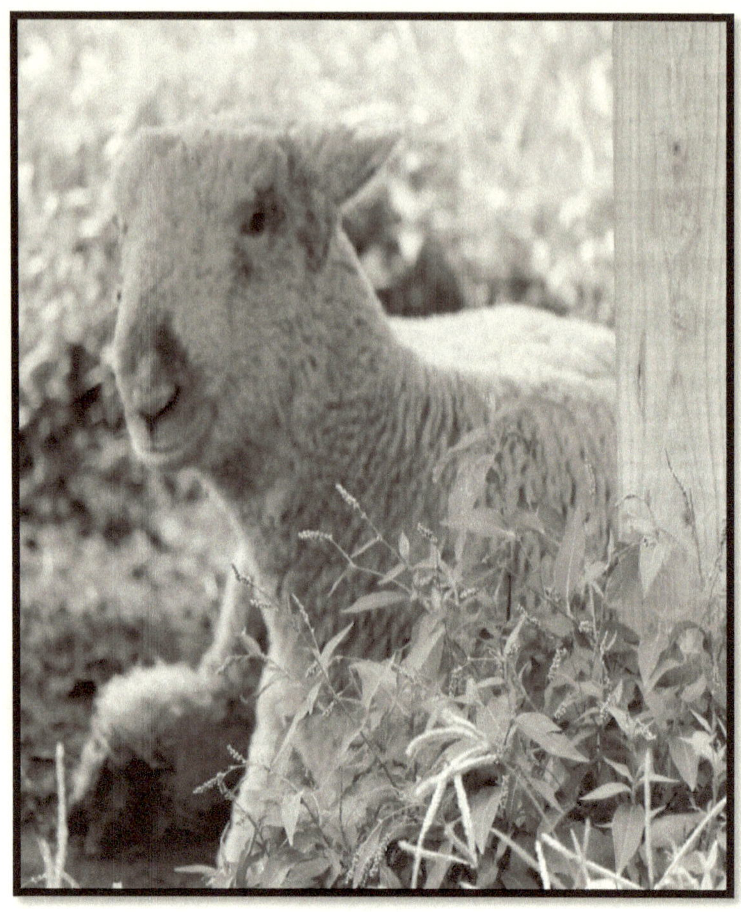

Relaxing

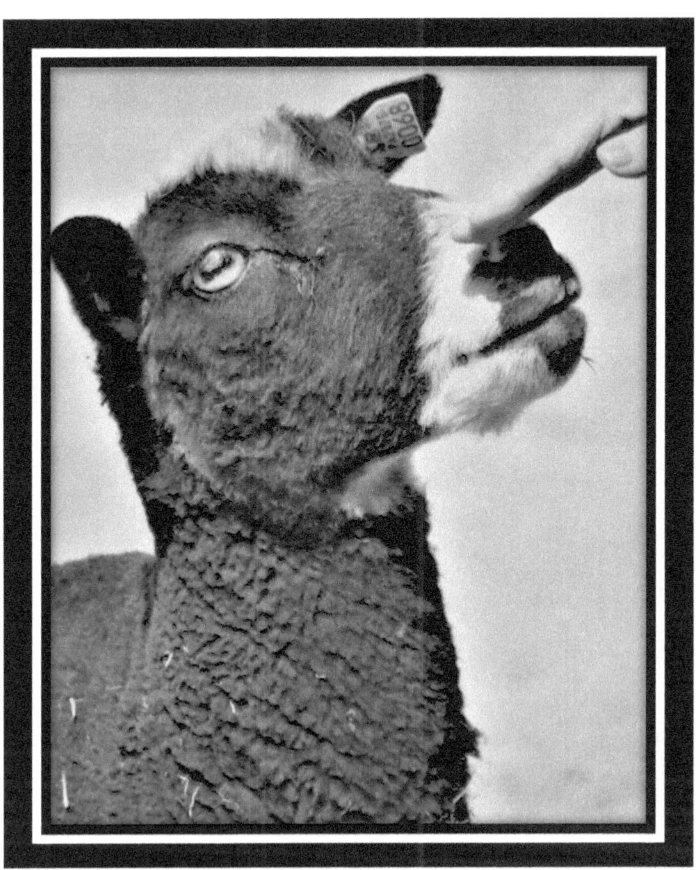

Friendly Pat On The Nose!

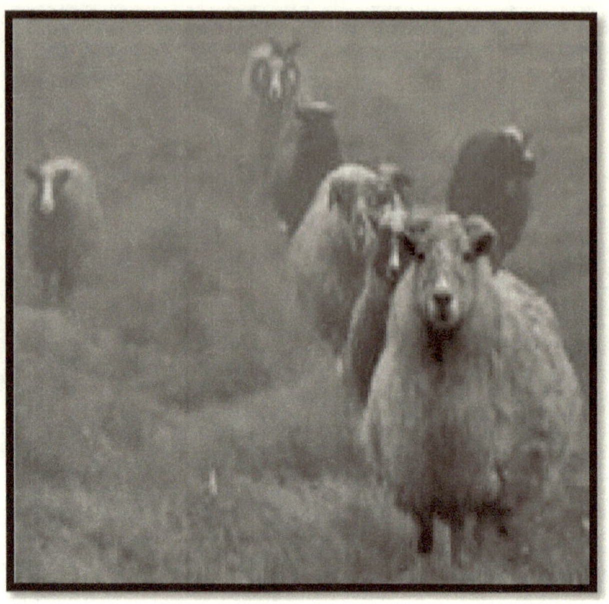

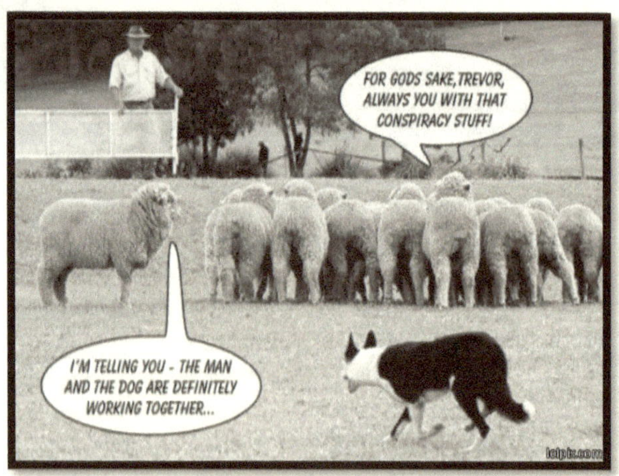
FOR GODS SAKE, TREVOR, ALWAYS YOU WITH THAT CONSPIRACY STUFF!
I'M TELLING YOU - THE MAN AND THE DOG ARE DEFINITELY WORKING TOGETHER...

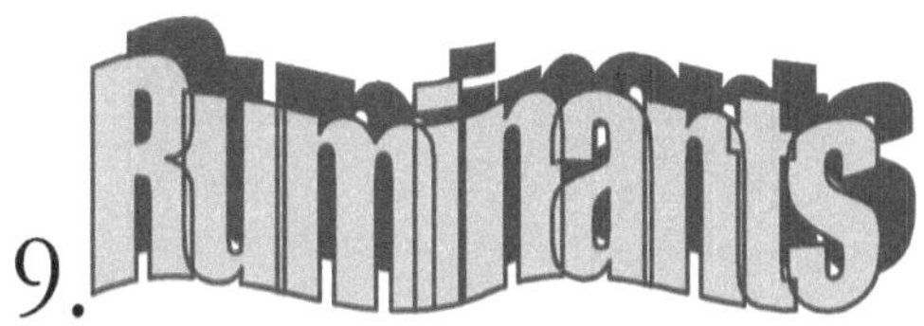

9. ruminant

[ˈro͞omənənt]

NOUN

1. an even-toed ungulate mammal that chews the cud regurgitated from its rumen. The ruminants comprise the cattle, sheep, antelopes, deer, giraffes, and their relatives.
2. a contemplative person; a person given to meditation.

ADJECTIVE

1. of or belonging to ruminants.

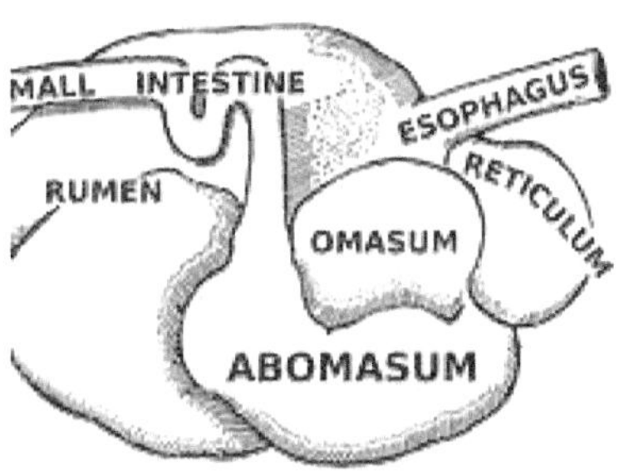

RUMINANTS ARE HERBIVOROUS MAMMALS THAT ARE ABLE TO ACQUIRE NUTRIENTS FROM PLANT-BASED FOOD BY FERMENTING IT IN A SPECIALIZED STOMACH PRIOR TO DIGESTION, THROUGH MICROBIAL ACTIONS. THE WORD "RUMINANT"

COMES FROM THE LATIN RUMINARE, WHICH MEANS "TO CHEW OVER AGAIN".

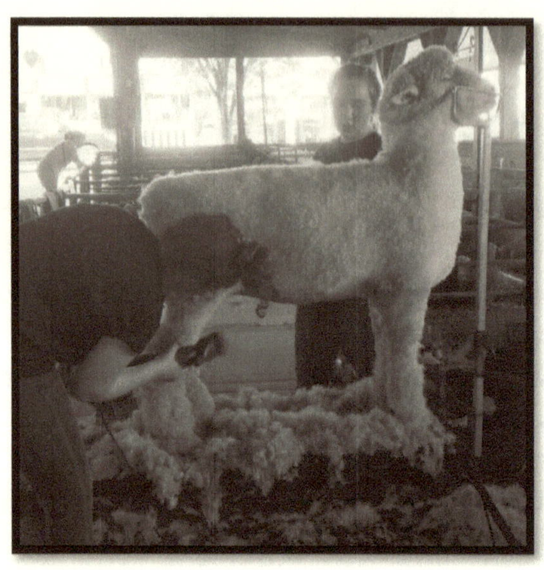

**WHY ARE EWE SPECIAL? YOU RUMINANT CREATURE
WITH A STRANGE TYPE OF STOMACH, A UNIQUE FEATURE!
CHEWING YOUR CUD IS WHAT YOU ARE GOOD AT !
YOU KEEP YOURSELF BUSY - CHEWING IS A STAT!
YOU CAN CHEW ALL DAY LONG WHEREVER YOU'RE AT!
IT LOOKS LIKE YOU'RE THINKING ABOUT HOW YOU SHOULD CHEW. IF YOU FIND SOMETHING DIFFERENT -IT SEEMS LIKE IT'S NEW.
RELAXING AND VIEWING TO TRY OUT A GRASS STEW!**

FOUR STOMACHS YOU HAVE AND THAT'S PRETTY NEAT.
JUST AS LONG AS YOU ARE ABLE TO FIND SOMETHING TO EAT!

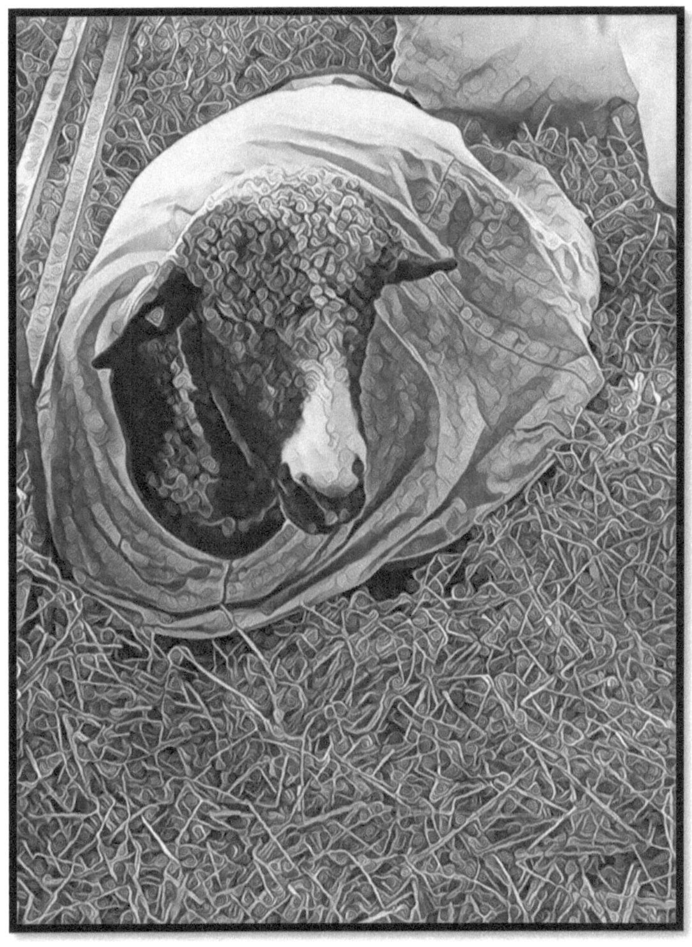

A ruminant is an even-toed, hoofed, four-legged mammal that eats grass and other

plants. Ruminants include domestic cattle (cows), sheep, goats, bison, buffalo, deer, antelopes, giraffes, and camels.

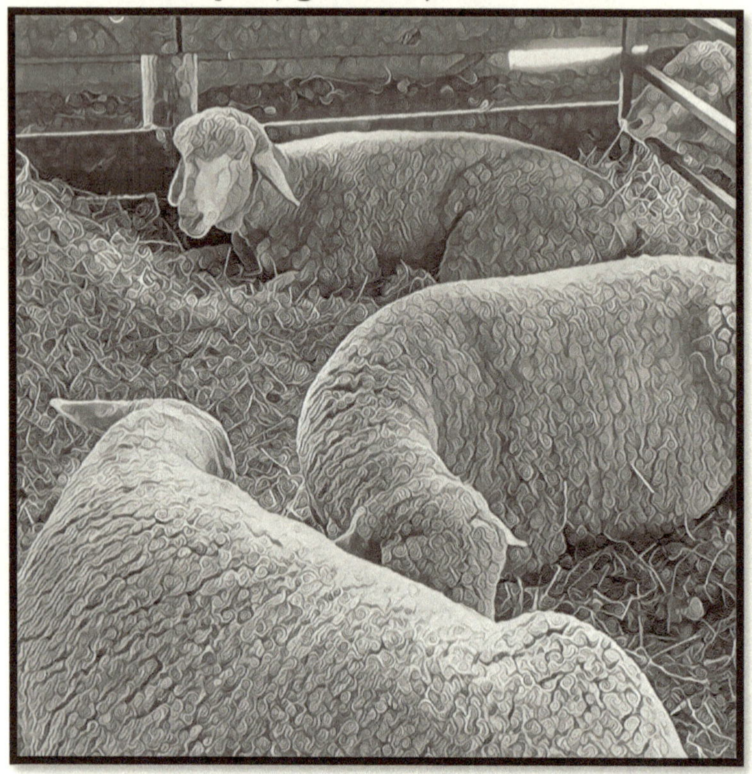

Maryland Sheep and Wool Festival

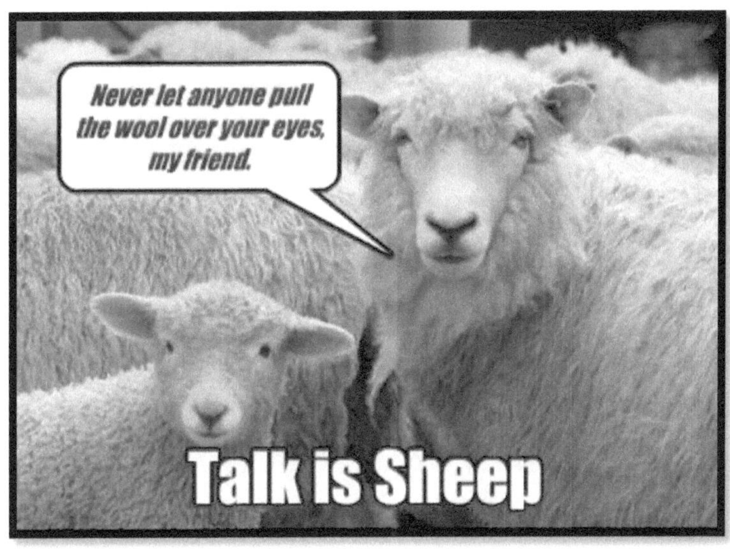

Talk is Sheep if you are a EWE!
The gossip keeps growing whatever you do!
Before ewe know it- the herd will be stirring to see if the gossip discussed keeps on growing.
Sometimes it is good and very entertaining, ewe chuckle ewe smurk so the audience is maintaining.
Ewe didn't realize ewe where the center of attention and before long the group is upset and starts blaming!
Ewe ate most of the feed and pushed the others away- so they were lucky to

get nourishment in the pen with the hay!
Ewe never realized they were upset
because ewe were so busy. Why are they
all snorting and have themselves in a
tizzy?
Oh well, that is life and it is survival of
the fittest. Ewe can't help it you are so
strong and happen to be the biggest.
So life goes on, get over it will ewe?
It's a sheep thing ewe know, nothing
new, it's just what ewe do!
Ewe are a work of art with your poses and
expressions.
Ewe are hard to figure out since ewe are
so good at posing for your sessions!
I take your picture when you look me in
the eye. Then ewe move to another spot
as ewe shake your head and sigh!
What is this ewe wonder - you keep
pointing at us, as ewe move around and
fuss?
The perfect photo? There is no such
thing, it is very subjective but it adds to
our bling!
Sheep art is always a ruminant thing
But keep taking our photos, they add to

our Zing!

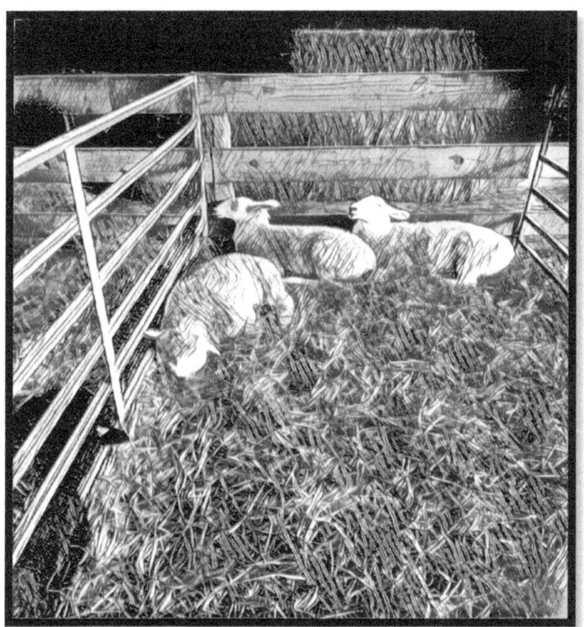

Nap Time At The Show - R.Dean

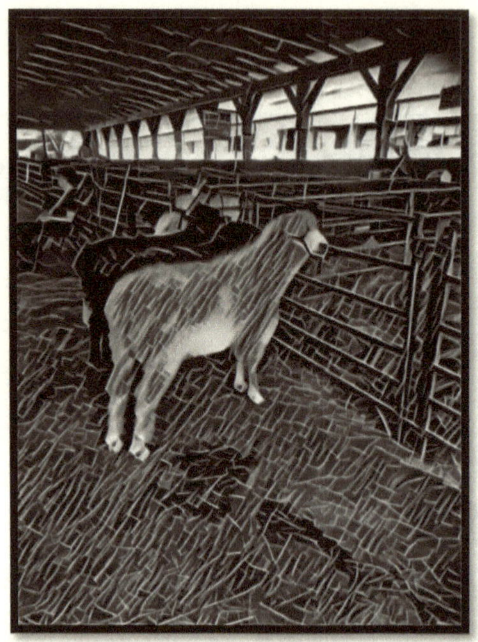

Abstract Ewes At The Fair -R.Dean

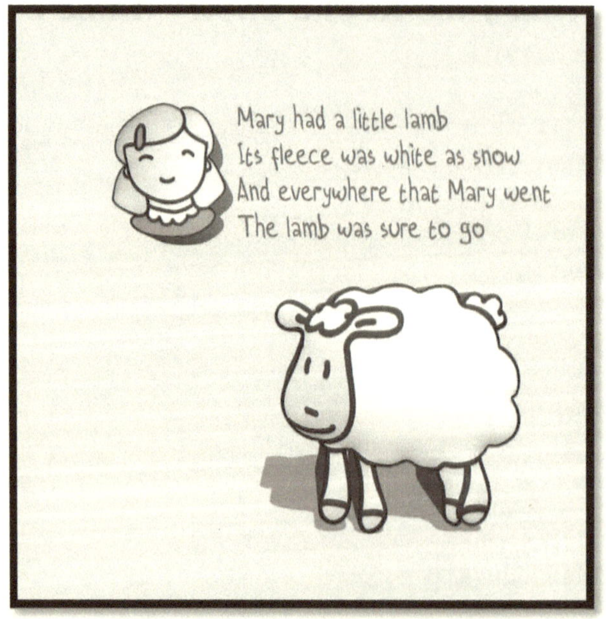

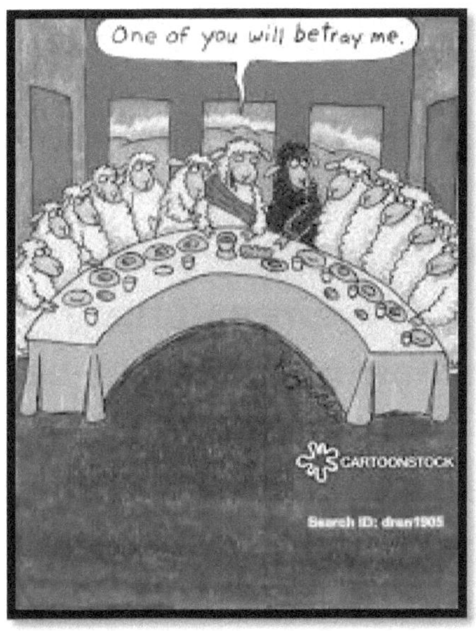
One of you will betray me.
CARTOONSTOCK
Search ID: dren1905

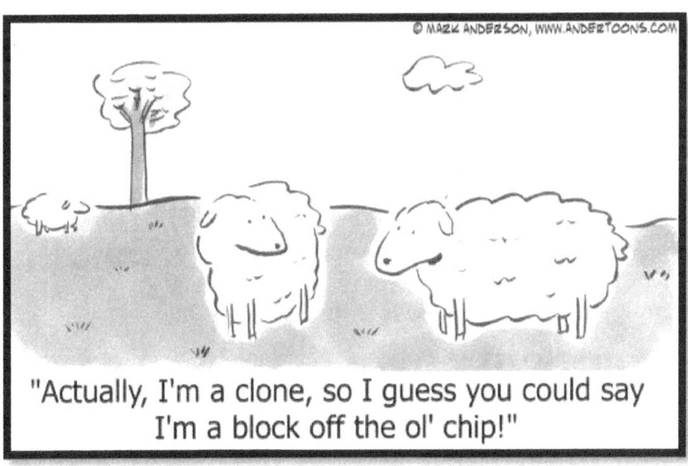
© MARK ANDERSON, WWW.ANDERTOONS.COM
"Actually, I'm a clone, so I guess you could say
I'm a block off the ol' chip!"

Ode To Sheep of Celtic Herd

Sheep of Celtic Herd, Ewe can be funny - really absurd!
Your faces can have such comical expressions
You vary their outputs but never show aggression.
Ewe have that curiosity thing going for you with your facial displays.
Ewe run for your food and chomp down on your hay.
In fact you can do this for hours each day.
It is so entertaining to watch you chew with delight
Ewe knock each other around to get the prime spots with fights!
Most of ewe simply move to another close spot.
You sneak in where there's an opening and you do that alot!
I enjoy watching these interactions and am always amused
When you have finished the lot, you lie down and you *snooze!*

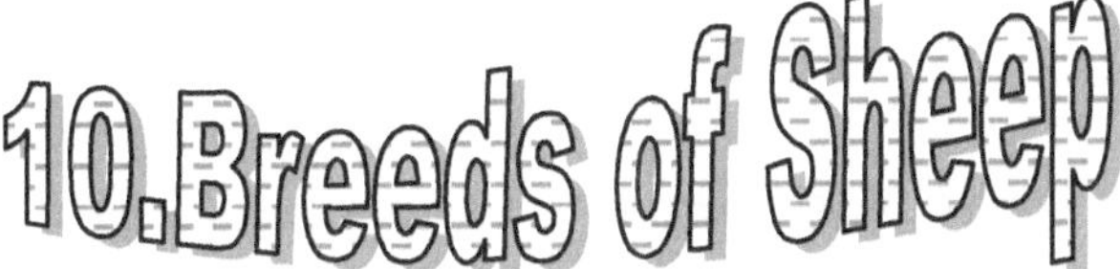

1. The *Merino* is one of the most relevant and economically influential breeds of sheep, much prized for its wool.

2. The *Suffolk* is a British breed of domestic sheep. It originated in the late eighteenth century in the area of Bury St. Edmunds in Suffolk

3. The *Icelandic* sheep is a breed of domestic sheep. The Icelandic breed is one of the Northern European short-tailed sheep, which exhibit a fluke-shaped, naturally short tail. The Icelandic is a mid-sized breed, generally short-legged and stocky, with face and legs free of wool.

4. *Dorper* sheep are South African-bred, first developed as a combination of the Blackhead Persian and the Dorset Horn.

5. The *Jacob* is a British breed of domestic sheep. It combines two characteristics unusual in sheep: it is piebald—dark-colored with areas of white wool—and it is often multi-horned. It most commonly has four horns.

6. *Katahdin* Sheep work very well in a variety of   situations as a low-maintenance, easy care sheep.

7. The *Southdown* is a small, dual-purpose English sheep, raised primarily for meat. The Southdown breed was originally bred by John Ellman of Glynde, near Lewes, East Sussex, about 200 years ago.

8. The *Border Leicester* is a British breed of sheep. It is a polled, long-wool sheep and is considered a dual-purpose breed as it is reared both for meat and for wool. The sheep are large but docile.

9. The *Scottish Blackface* sheep is a breed of domestic sheep from Scotland. It is the most common breed of domestic sheep in the United Kingdom.. Exact origins of this breed are unknown.

10. The roots of the *Shetland Sheep* go back over a thousand years, probably to sheep brought to the Shetland Islands by Viking settlers. They belong to the Northern European short-tailed group which also contains the Finnsheep, Norwegian Spaelsau, Icelandics, Romanovs and others.

There are many other breeds of sheep, but that is another story!

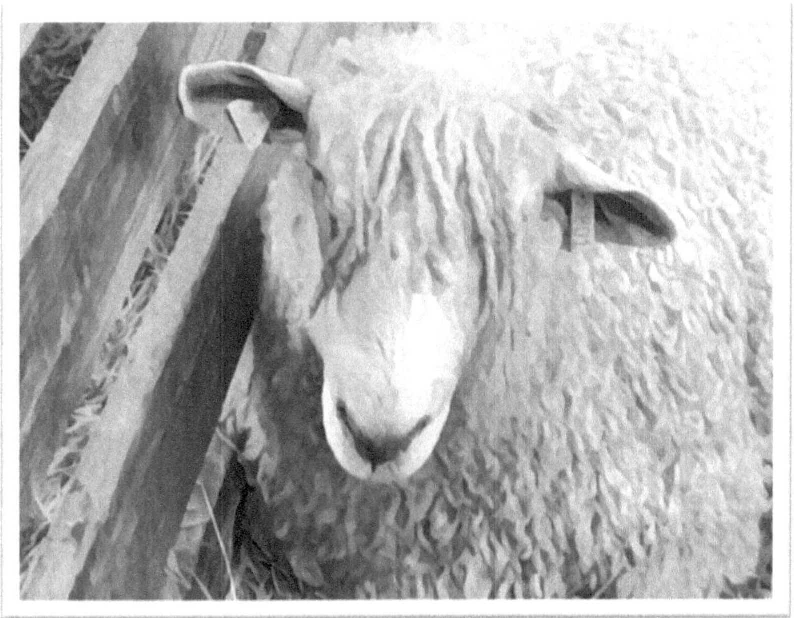

Photo by R.Dean

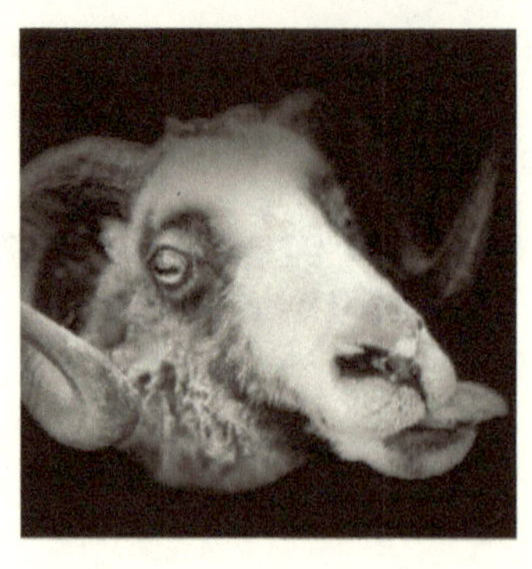

ABOUT THE AUTHOR

Roxanne Dean has been raising Scottish Sheep for over twenty years. Her first Shetland ewe was Sheila, a black sheep with a friendly temperament who later became the star in many of her books. The Scottish Blackface sheep were added when her daughter became involved in 4H and took home her first ewe from the Maryland Sheep and Wool Festival at the Howard County Fairgrounds in Maryland. Roxanne has 12 books out about her sheep and dogs along with a photography book about Birds and Nature. Photography is her other hobby and she has won many awards from The Sheep of Celtic Herd.